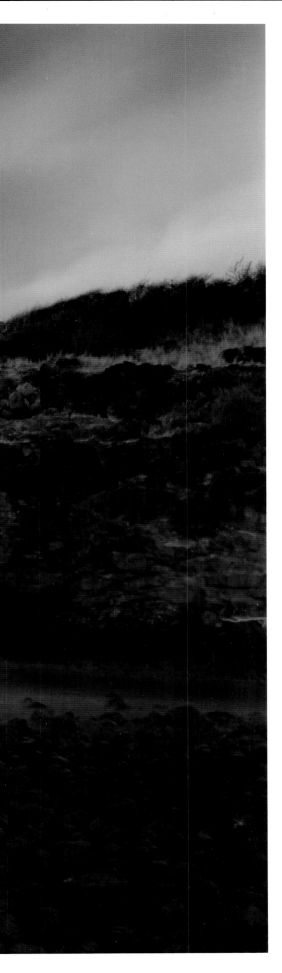

Hoʻolaʻa ʻia kēia i ka poʻe o mua aʻe nei nāna i hoʻoulu i ka mahalo a me ke aloha ʻāina i kēia hanana, a i ka poʻe e ola nei e kāʻana mau aku ana i ka nani me ka pono o ka nohona ʻōiwi o ka Hawaiʻi me ke kūlia mau ʻana e hoʻōla hou iā Kahoʻolawe

Dedicated to those who have passed on, who inspired this generation to respect and care for the land. And to those who live on sharing the richness and beauty of the native Hawaiian lifestyle and persist in the work to bring life to Kahoʻolawe.

ʻO Wākea noho iā Papahānaumoku,

Wākea lived with Papa, begetter of islands.

Hānau ʻo Hawaiʻi, he moku,

Born was Hawaiʻi, an island,

Hānau ʻo Maui, he moku.

Born was Maui, an island.

Hoʻi hou ʻo Wākea, noho iā Hoʻohokukalani.

Wākea left and lived with Hoʻohokukalani.

Hānau ʻo Molokaʻi, he moku,

Born was Molokaʻi, an island,

Hānau ʻo Lānaʻi ka ʻula, he moku.

Born was red Lānaʻi, an island.

Liliʻōpūpunalua ʻo Papa iā Hoʻohokukalani.

Papa became jealous at the partnership with Hoʻohokukalani.

Hoʻi hou ʻo Papa, noho iā Wākea.

Papa went and lived with Wākea.

Hānau ʻo Oʻahu, he moku,

Born was Oʻahu, an island,

Hānau ʻo Kauaʻi, he moku,

Born was Kauaʻi, an island,

Hānau ʻo Niʻihau, he moku,

Born was Niʻihau, an island,

He ʻula a ʻo Kahoʻolawe.

A red one was Kahoʻolawe.

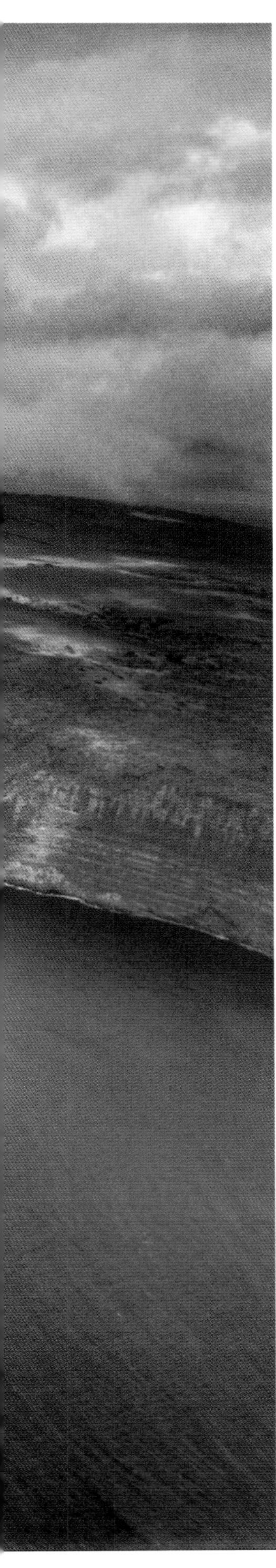

KAHOʻOLAWE

Nā Leo o Kanaloa

CHANTS AND STORIES OF KAHOʻOLAWE

PHOTOGRAPHS BY
WAYNE LEVIN
ROWLAND B. REEVE
FRANCO SALMOIRAGHI
DAVID ULRICH

ʻAi Pōhaku Press: Honolulu

ON PAGES VIII–IX:
Over the millennia, ocean swells have cut away at Kaho'olawe's southern shore, exposing the bedded layers of lava that built the island and carving out such features as the bay of Kamohio, the sea-stack of 'Ale'ale, and the offshore islet of Pu'ukoa'e. Behind the rampart of sea cliffs, the island's central plateau stretches away toward the prominent cindercone of Moa'ulaiki.

For information on how to obtain copies of this book,
please contact: 'Ai Pōhaku Press
c/o Native Books
P.O. Box 37095
Honolulu, Hawai'i 96837-0095
808–845–8949 or 1–800–887–7751

LIBRARY OF CONGRESS CATALOG CARD NO. 95–080383
ISBN 1–883528–01–1 CLOTHBOUND EDITION
ISBN 1–883528–02–X PAPERBOUND EDITION

Directed by Barbara Pope, Rowland B. Reeve, and Maile Meyer
Edited by Nelson Foster
Hawaiian-language editing by Puakea Nogelmeier
Designed and produced by Barbara Pope Book Design
Printed and bound in Hong Kong

Contents

Aunty Emma DeFries was a guiding force in the movement to stop the bombing of Kaho'olawe and recover the island for the people of Hawai'i. Here she sits in reflection on the beach at Hakioawa during the Protect Kaho'olawe 'Ohana's first legally permitted visit to Kaho'olawe in 1976.

Foreword

NOA EMMETT ALULI, M.D.
PROTECT KAHOʻOLAWE ʻOHANA

Aunty Barbara Hanchett, Aunty Lani Kapuni, Aunty Clara Ku, Aunty Mary Lee, Aunty Rose Wainui (front), and other Hawaiian kūpuna *(elders) supported and lent inspiration to the movement to reclaim Kahoʻolawe. At their feet are* niu *(coconut palms) to plant on the island and other* hoʻokupu *(offerings).*

Hawaiians of generations past loved the land very much. We call this *aloha ʻāina.* Whether it was a rainbow, the wind, the rain, whether it was the volcano, a stream, the ocean—all of them were understood as forms and energies of the gods, and Hawaiians prayed to them. Hawaiians made sure that the land was healthy, that it was cared for, that it was respected. They made sure that everything stayed in balance. As they did that for the land, they did it for themselves, their families, their communities.

On Kahoʻolawe, we've been able to live together as Hawaiians. We've been able to practice the religion and to carry on the traditions we've learned from our *kūpuna,* our elders. In doing this, we connect to the land, and we connect to the gods. We call them back to the land and back to our lives. This affects us when we return to our home islands. That same respect for the land has been carried back to all the other islands, and that connection to the culture is expressed in our families and in the work we do with our communities. As we bring all those important cultural practices back into everyday experience, we begin to pay more attention to our health, for example. We begin to look after our *kūpuna* the way they looked after us when we were young. What we've seen and felt and learned on Kahoʻolawe filters into our lives in many ways.

As we've continued to take people to Kahoʻolawe and to educate them, people have begun to look upon Kahoʻolawe as a symbol and a model. Seeing this success in taking care of the land, they've begun to feel that it's native Hawaiians' responsibility to protect the land throughout the islands. The only way to do that is through a native, sovereign government that is based on respect for the land and stewardship of it. We believe that the work to heal the island of Kahoʻolawe has helped heal the soul of our people and that it will continue to do so. As we work to restore the island, each time we pick up a stone that has fallen from a cultural site, we pick ourselves up as a people. We lay the foundation for a nation.

The key thing to remember is that there's always going to be more work to do. We commit for generations, not just for careers. We set things up now so that they'll be carried on. We look ahead together so that many of us share the same vision and dream. This *ʻohana* process, this extended-family process, is the main lesson for everybody. We can make a difference collectively, cumulatively, over time. We need to charge ahead, but we also need to be patient. And we need to have fun and to respect, look out for, and care for one another.

Kahoʻolawe: Nā Leo o Kanaloa evokes the feeling of being on the island. Its words and photographs reveal the spirit, the power, the sensations that we experience there. *Nā leo,* the voices, of Kanaloa take many forms—the wind, the pounding waves, the smell of the ocean, the heat, the visions that come to mind. Over the past twenty years, the Protect Kahoʻolawe ʻOhana has grown into the family for Kahoʻolawe. Each of us, in some way, has heard the varied voices of the island, has felt the pull to come back to care for it, has kept being drawn into a tighter connection with the island and with each other. We've each had a feeling, a response, a reaction, a calling to this island and to the cause of helping to save

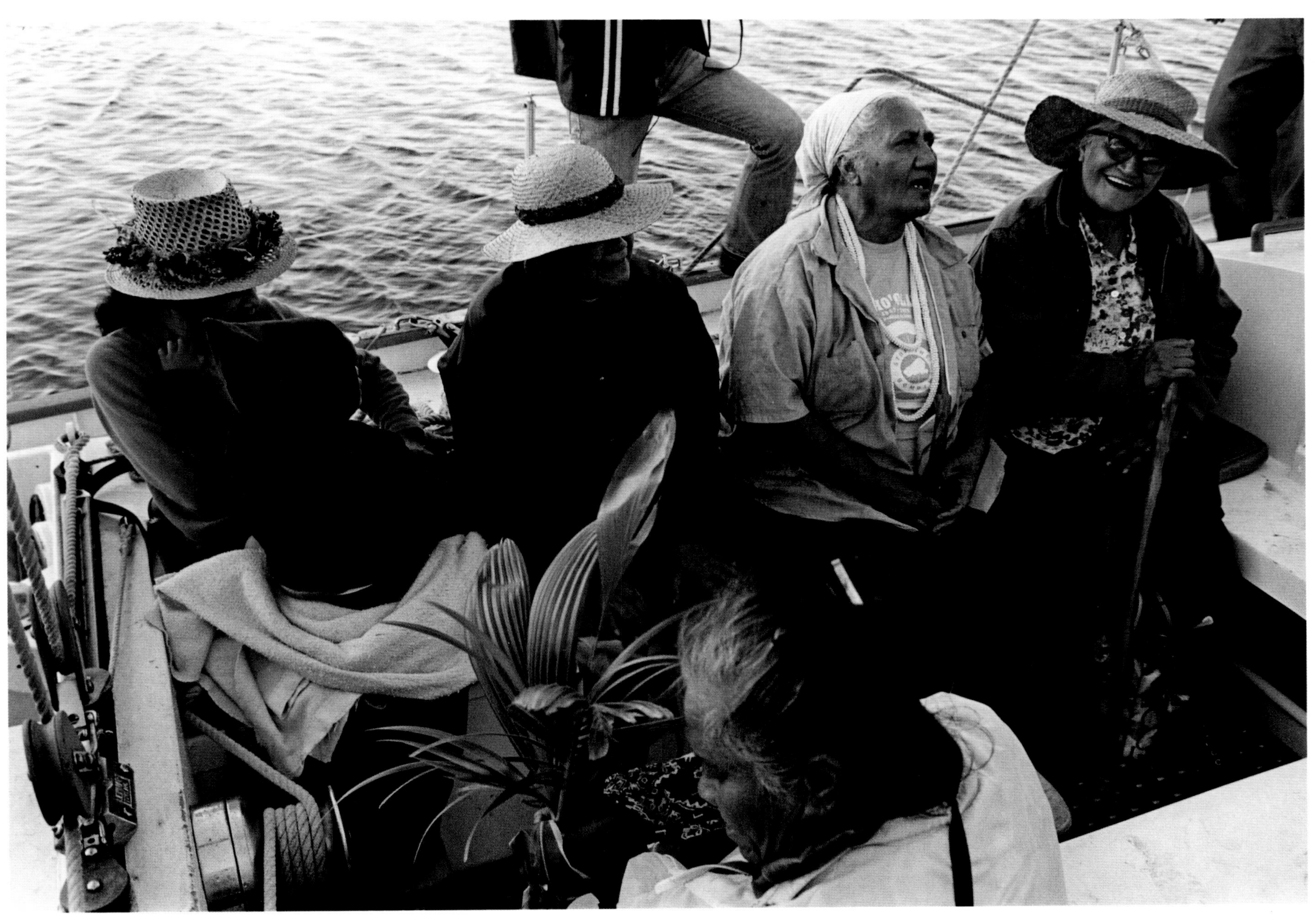

it and helping to lay a firmer, more secure foundation for the generations ahead. To our next generations we say, Go with the spirit. Take the challenge. Learn something. Give back. Learn something from this book. Feel something from this book. Go visit the many places of the ancestors, not just Kahoʻolawe. Make the connection to our ancestors on all our islands. Kahoʻolawe is a good starting place because it doesn't have the distractions of the fast life—but don't stop there. Be open, feel your *naʻau,* let yourself be guided by our *kānaka makua,* our *kūpuna,* our *ʻaumākua,* and our *akua.* Hear and feel those voices.

Introduction

ROWLAND B. REEVE

The twenty-year struggle to reclaim and restore the island of Kahoʻolawe has made its name familiar to anyone in Hawaiʻi who reads a local paper or tunes in the evening news. Yet the island itself remains oddly unknown to most Hawaiʻi residents, not to mention the millions who come here each year as visitors. Public perceptions of Kahoʻolawe have been shaped mainly by headlines and news clips, by the patter of flight attendants, and by the images that photographers and TV camera crews have captured during quick trips to the island. A few more than five thousand of us—under one percent of the resident population—have ever set foot on Kahoʻolawe. Most know it better as a political symbol than as an actual place, and in the public eye it remains small and lifeless and remote, a barren land of scarred, red earth and windblown dust.

This book is the first of two volumes intended to present a truer, far more complete portrait of Kahoʻolawe, one that reveals the current look and feel of the island as well as the story of its past. We hope these books will bring Kahoʻolawe alive for those who have not yet had the opportunity to see the island for themselves—to walk its coastline or explore its hills, to experience its quiet beauty and feel its *mana.* While the second volume will furnish a comprehensive account of Kahoʻolawe's history, in this first one we have stood aside and let the island itself speak as directly as possible, through the voices of Hawaiian poets, historians, and storytellers and through the lenses of four photographers.

Before the changes brought by Western contact, each inhabited island in the Hawaiian chain had its own body of *mele* (chants) and *moʻolelo* (accounts, legends, folktales). These traditions were treasured and passed down by word of mouth from generation to generation, for they contained the lore of the islands and the history of their people. As Kahoʻolawe's indigenous population dwindled, it lost the greatest repository of its traditions, and today only those *mele* and *moʻolelo* survive that were set down in writing or perpetuated by families living elsewhere. Nearly all of the Kahoʻolawe traditions now known appear in the pages that follow, brought together for the first time in a single publication. They range from complete stories to brief excerpts drawn from epic narratives.

The richness and diversity of these surviving traditions suggest how bountiful Kahoʻolawe's original stock of *mele* and *moʻolelo* must have been, and their words indicate how deeply the island was woven into the fabric of Hawaiian society. Prior to its imposed isolation in the mid-nineteenth century, Kahoʻolawe was an integral part of the Hawaiian world. It appears alongside the other major islands in the great chants of creation describing the birth of Hawaiʻi, features prominently in accounts of early voyaging chiefs, and plays important roles in legends and folktales. These traditions tell us a great deal about the island's past and provide a sense of what Kahoʻolawe meant to the people who inhabited it. To them the island was a child of Papa and Wākea, the earth and the sky; a home to gods as well as humans; a place at once utterly unique and closely related to the other islands of the chain.

Unearthing and assembling Kahoʻolawe's long-scattered *mele* and *moʻolelo* has been a lengthy process. In the early 1980s, archivist Carol Silva compiled the first collection of traditional materials relating to the island, and this volume owes a great deal to her pioneering efforts. Subsequent researchers have recovered additional material from a variety of sources, including early Hawaiian-language newspapers, unpublished manuscripts, and private letters now housed in library archives. It is possible that still more material waits in some yet untapped archive or in the memories of island families. If so, we hope publication of this volume will hasten its disclosure.

Though the main emphasis of this text is material from Kahoʻolawe's past, it also contains a selection of contemporary chants. Hawaiian oral tradition, like Hawaiian culture as a whole, did not cease with the arrival of Captain Cook. As has been true for countless generations, talented individuals today are maintaining, and continuing to pass down, the knowledge and skills needed to create chants in the ancient manner. For a number of these present-day *haku mele* (composers), Kahoʻolawe has been a source of deep inspiration. Their chants express what the island has come to represent to many contemporary Hawaiians: over the past two decades, this "Island of Death," as it was once called, has become a place of refuge and cultural rebirth.

In order to be faithful to the *mele* and *moʻolelo* and, at the same time, to make them widely accessible, we have chosen to publish them bilingually, giving each first in Hawaiian and then in an English translation. Most were recorded at a time when Hawaiian was written without the *ʻokina* (glottal stop) and the *kahakō* (macron) that have since become standard in Hawaiian orthography. Wishing to add these elements, which indicate the pronunciation of a word, and frequently its meaning, we asked Hawaiian-language scholar Puakea Nogelmeier to review and update the Hawaiian texts. We are profoundly grateful for his generous assistance. Puakea has also reviewed Kahoʻolawe's place-names, adding *ʻokina* and *kahakō* to those whose pronunciation and meaning are clear. The remaining place-names are unmarked, except in contemporary chants, where the composers have rendered names in accord with their own understanding of the meaning.

In presenting English versions of these texts, wherever possible we have made use of existing translations, modifying them only as necessary to clarify obscure passages or to correct errors. In the case of old traditions never before translated, we again called upon the expertise of Puakea Nogelmeier, and he has rendered them into English for us. Readers who wish to examine the original Hawaiian materials or previous English translations in unadapted form will find source information for each text listed in the back of the book.

Like any literature, Hawaiian oral tradition is filled with allusions to gods, people, places, and events specific to the culture and place. Such allusions play an especially important role in *mele,* for poetic custom dictates that the power of a chant resides, to a large degree, in its ability to evoke many levels of meaning and association. In composing chants, *haku mele* have employed a rich vocabulary of cultural metaphors as well, and they often show less concern for conveying literal information than for expressing the essence of things through imagery. While these allusions and metaphors are readily recognizable to people well-versed in the culture, they are unfamiliar to most modern readers, and for this reason, we have noted and explained the most important of them in headnotes accompanying the translations. At the back of the book, we also provide a map of the island and a brief chronology that, until the companion volume is published, will help readers identify names, events, and places mentioned in the text.

To eliminate another source of potential confusion, it is important to note that the chants and stories refer to Kahoʻolawe by a number of different names. (In the preface to "Oli Kūhohonu o Kahoʻolawe mai nā Kūpuna mai," Harry Mitchell lists these names and gives his own interpretation of them.) The most prominent of the island's old names is

Kanaloa, the name under which Kahoʻolawe appears in *mele koʻihonua,* the chiefly genealogical chants that describe the island's creation. Kahoʻolawe shares this name with one of the major Hawaiian deities, a god deeply associated with the sea and with voyaging. Many of the traditions found in this volume link Kahoʻolawe to the god Kanaloa and to his various *kinolau,* or physical manifestations. The name Kanaloa also says something about the character of Kahoʻolawe, for as an adjective *kanaloa* means "firm, immovable, unconquerable"—qualities that the island has demonstrated throughout its history. Since echoes of this ancient name resound throughout the book, we have subtitled it *Nā Leo o Kanaloa, the Voices of Kanaloa.*

Kahoʻolawe speaks in this book not only through its oral traditions but also through images by four local photographers—Wayne Levin, Franco Salmoiraghi, David Ulrich, and myself (specific photo credits are listed in an appendix). Together we were given the opportunity to visit and photograph Kahoʻolawe repeatedly over a two-year period between 1992 and 1994. In the course of that time, we were able to witness seasonal changes in the island's landscape, to see it in a variety of lights and moods, and to travel to many of its *wahi pana,* its noted and storied places. The photographs resulting from these visits form a visual record of Kahoʻolawe at this critical juncture in its history, when its abuse by the United States military has ended and it has been restored to those who cherish it and will care for it. Complementing this set of photographs is a small group of earlier images documenting important moments in the movement to revive the life of the island. The first of these date back to 1976, when Franco Salmoiraghi accompanied the Protect Kahoʻolawe ʻOhana during its first permitted landing on the island. Others were taken on a subsequent trip in 1979 and at the 1987 Makahiki ceremony, part of the ʻOhana's ongoing effort to reestablish on Kahoʻolawe the religious rituals that were central to the lives of its original inhabitants. Several of these early photographs depict sensitive subjects, and we have consulted with ʻOhana leaders and cultural authorities about presenting them here. The same holds for recent photographs of religious sites. We hope we have treated them appropriately.

As we have worked to bring this book to press, we have often been reminded of the many groups and individuals who contributed their time and expertise to help make it a reality. We are tremendously grateful for their help. Above all, we owe an immense debt of gratitude to the Protect Kahoʻolawe ʻOhana, whose members over the years have worked tirelessly to reclaim and restore the island. Without their support and guidance, this book would not exist. We are also indebted to the Kahoʻolawe Island Conveyance Commission and to its successor, the Kahoʻolawe Island Reserve Commission, both of which assisted us in obtaining access to Kahoʻolawe, as well as to the representatives of the United States Navy who provided us with lodging and transportation during many of our sojourns on the island.

Those who have the privilege of spending much time on Kahoʻolawe tend to be deeply affected by the experience. What it is that we find so moving is hard to express. Perhaps it is the island's physical beauty, its mingled sense of tragedy and hope, or the powerful, lingering presence of *ka poʻe kahiko,* the people of old. Though the printed page can never fully convey the *mana* of Kahoʻolawe, the words and images of this book may at least offer a sense of the island's breadth, beauty, and spirit. We hope the voices that speak through these pages will deepen your knowledge and love not only of Kahoʻolawe but of all Hawaiʻi, and that they may inspire you to continue the struggle to protect and preserve *ke ea o ka ʻāina,* the life of the land.

This contemporary lele *(offering platform) stands on the northwest ridge of Hakioawa valley, overlooking the Hale o Papa (women's temple). Kahoʻolawe has become a center for the revival of traditional Hawaiian religious practices, and the Hale o Papa is one of several religious sites in Hakioawa that have been cleared and rededicated. Another, the Hale Mua (men's temple), stands on the opposite ridge.*

Kahoʻolawe

Nā Leo o Kanaloa

THE VOICES OF KANALOA

Preceding page ⟜
The crest of Moa'ulaiki offers a panoramic view of Kaho'olawe as well as the channels and islands that encircle it. Northeastward from the peak, the vista encompasses the 'Alalākeiki channel, the mountains of west Maui, and the more distant hills of Moloka'i. Traditions suggest that Moa'ulaiki was once the site of a school for astronomy and navigation. In more recent times, an altar platform has been erected where offerings are made to the god Lono at the close of the annual Makahiki season.

These petroglyphs on the upper slopes of Moa'ulanui are among over four hundred rock carvings so far discovered on Kaho'olawe. While most of the island's petroglyphs depict readily recognizable human and animal figures, others, like these images, are more complex and harder to interpret.

Ka Mele a Pākuʻi

THE CHANT OF PĀKUʻI

ʻO Wākeakahikoluamea,

Wākea, son of Kahikoluamea, was the husband;

ʻO Papa, ʻo Papahānaumoku ka wahine,

Papa, who gives birth to islands was the wife.

Hānau Kahikikū, Kahikimoe,

Kahiki of the rising sun and Kahiki of the setting sun were born.

Hānau Keʻāpapanui,

Born were the foundation strata.

Hānau Keʻāpapalani,

Born were the heavenly strata.

Hānau Hawaiʻi;

Born was Hawaiʻi,

Ka moku makahiapo,

The first-born island,

Ka makahiapo a lāua.

The first-born child of them

ʻO Wākea lāua ʻo Kāne,

Of Wākea together with Kāne,

ʻO Papa, ʻo Walinuʻu, ka wahine.

Of Papa, Walinuʻu, the wife.

Hoʻokauhua Papa i ka moku,

Papa conceived an island,

These lines form the beginning of a lengthy *mele koʻihonua,* a genealogical chant honoring the warrior chief Kamehameha I. The *mele* is said to have been composed by Pākuʻi, a renowned chanter and high-ranking *kahuna* (priest) of the eighteenth century. Traditionally composed solely for members of the chiefly class, *mele koʻihonua* served as emblems of power, affirming the stature of a ruling *aliʻi* (chief) by tracing his ancestry back to the gods. These *mele* are among the loftiest forms of Hawaiian poetry, and their verses are crowded with historic allusions and *kaona* (hidden meanings). Like many *mele koʻihonua,* the chant of Pākuʻi begins at the dawn of time, and its opening passage recounts the birth of the Hawaiian Islands.

The verses given here place the three southernmost islands —Hawaiʻi, Mauiloa (long Maui), and Kanaloa (Kahoʻolawe)—in the context of the creation of Kahiki (southern Polynesia). All were born of the gods Papa and Wākea, the earth and the sky. The name Mololani, which also appears in the sequence of islands, is difficult to interpret. It does not refer to Molokaʻi, whose birth is recorded later in the poem, and Molokini seems unlikely since the islet was not known to be an "important one" to the gods. The word *mololani* itself means "carefully nursed" and may simply describe either Maui or Kahoʻolawe.

Hoʻīloli iā Maui,

Was ill with morning sickness from Maui.

Hānau Mauiloa he moku;

Born was Mauiloa, an island,

I hānau ʻia he alo lani,

Born with a heavenly presence.

He uʻilani, uʻilani,

A heavenly beauty, heavenly beauty,

Hei kapa lau māewa.

Was caught in the swaying kapa.

He nui Mololani no Kū, no Lono,

Mololani—an important one to Kū, to Lono,

No Kāne mā, lāua ʻo Kanaloa.

To Kāne, and also to Kanaloa —

Hānau kapu ke kuakoko

Was born during sacred pains.

Kaʻahea Papa iā Kanaloa, he moku,

Papa was prostrate with Kanaloa, an island,

I hānau ʻia he pūnua, he naiʻa,

Who was born as a young bird, as a porpoise,

He keiki ia na Papa i hānau,

A child that Papa gave birth to.

Haʻalele Papa, hoʻi i Kahiki,

Then Papa left and returned to Kahiki,

Hoʻi a Kahiki Kapakapakaua. . . .

Went back to Kahiki of Kapakapakaua. . . .

Schools of spinner dolphins can be seen almost daily resting and playing in the sheltered waters of Hana-kanaiʻa (Hana-ka-naiʻa—bay of the dolphin) on Kahoʻolawe's southwest coast. The naiʻa *is considered one of the* kinolau*—the physical manifestations—of the god Kanaloa, for whom the island was named.*

ʻO ka Moʻolelo o Kāne a me Kanaloa

THE TRADITION OF KĀNE AND KANALOA

Ua ʻōlelo pinepine ʻia ma ka moʻolelo kaʻao a ma nā pule, a ma nā mele a ka poʻe kahiko a pau, mai Kahiki mai ke akua, a mai ka lewa lani mai, a no ka lani mai. ʻO ka moʻolelo o Kāne a me Kanaloa, a ʻo lāua paha nā kahu akua mua i hiki mai i Hawaiʻi nei, a no ko lāua mana ua kapa ʻia lāua he mau akua. A ua kapa mua ʻia ʻo Kahoʻolawe ʻo Kanaloa ka inoa, no ka hiki mua ʻana mai ma Kealaikahiki. Mai Kahoʻolawe aku lāua a hiki i Kahikinui, na lāua i wāwahi ka loko iʻa a Kanaloa, aia ma Lualaʻilua; na lāua ka wai o Kou ma Kaupō.

In the traditions and prayers and chants of ka poʻe kahiko *[the people of old], it is often said that the gods came from Kahiki, from the upper realms,* lewa lani, *and from the heavens,* lani. *According to the* moʻolelo *[tradition] of Kāne and Kanaloa, they were perhaps the first guardian gods to come here to Hawaiʻi, and because of their* mana *[spiritual power] they were called gods. Kahoʻolawe was first named Kanaloa for their having first come there by way of Kealaikahiki. From Kahoʻolawe the two went to Kahikinui, Maui, where they opened up the fishpond of Kanaloa at Lualaʻilua; from them came the water of Kou at Kaupō.*

This account of Kāne and Kanaloa's arrival from Kahiki appeared in a series of articles that Hawaiian historian Samuel Kamakau wrote in the 1860s for the newspaper *Ka Nūpepa Kūʻokoʻa.* It was translated into English a century later by Mary Kawena Pukui. Though the place-name Kahiki is commonly translated as Tahiti, this word was used by the early Hawaiians to refer to any of the numerous islands of southern Polynesia and, by inference, to any foreign land. The name Kealaikahiki (Ke-ala-i-kahiki—the pathway to distant lands) belongs both to the westernmost tip of Kahoʻolawe and to the channel that flows along its northern coast, separating it from the nearby island of Lānaʻi. Numerous traditions speak of Kealaikahiki as the point of arrival and departure for canoes journeying to and from the southern islands.

Like the nai'a, *the endangered* honu *(green sea turtle) is a* kinolau *of Kanaloa. Sea turtle populations have begun to reestablish themselves in the waters around Kaho'olawe, and recently* honu *have been seen laying eggs in the sands of the island's western beaches.*

The westernmost tip of Kahoʻolawe, known as Laeokealaikahiki (point of the pathway to Kahiki), was an important navigational landmark for early voyagers traveling to and from the islands of southern Polynesia. Here the gods Kāne and Kanaloa are said to have first stepped ashore in Hawaiʻi.

Ea mai Hawai'inuiākea

THEN AROSE HAWAIʻINUIĀKEA

Ea mai Hawaiʻinuiākea,

Then arose Hawaiʻinuiākea [great expansive Hawaiʻi],

Ea mai loko, mai loko mai o ka pō.

Arose from inside, from within the darkness.

Puka mai ka moku, ka ʻāina,

Then appeared the island, the land,

Ka lālani ʻāina o Nuʻumea,

The row of islands of Nuʻumea,

Ka pae ʻāina i Kūkuluokahiki.

The group of islands on the borders of Kahiki.

Hānau ʻo Maui, he moku, he ʻāina,

Maui was born, an island, a land,

Na Kama, ʻo Kamalālāwalu e noho.

A dwelling place for Kama, Kamalālāwalu.

Na Kuluwaiea ʻo Haumea, he kāne,

To Kuluwaiea as the husband of Haumea,

Na Hinanuialana, he wahine

To Hinanuialana as the wife

Loaʻa Molokaʻi, ke akua, he kahuna,

Was born Molokaʻi, a god, a priest,

He pualena no Nuʻumea,

The first morning light for Nuʻumea.

The traditions of early Hawaiʻi offer varying accounts of how the islands came into being. In this version, from a long *mele koʻihonua* composed about the same date as "Ka Mele a Pākuʻi" and likewise dedicated to Kamehameha I, the islands are said to have been conceived by several different sets of parents. Kahoʻolawe here is born to Keaukanai and Walinuʻu, a woman of Hōlani. Both Hōlani and Nuʻumea are mythical lands in distant Kahiki. The chant describes Lānaʻi as an adopted child and Kahoʻolawe as "he lōpā," a tenant farmer, suggesting their dependent relationship to larger Maui. Tradition attributes "Ea mai Hawaiʻinuiākea" to the priest Kahakuikamoana.

Kū mai ke aliʻi, ka lani.

Here stands the royal one, the heavenly one,

Ka haluku wai ea o Kahiki.

The life-giving water-drops from Kahiki.

Loaʻa Lānaʻi he keiki hoʻokama.

Lānaʻi was born, an adopted child.

Na Keaukanai i moe aku,

It was Keaukanai who had married,

Moe iā Walinuʻu o Hōlani, he keakea kapu no Uluhina,

Had married Walinuʻu from Hōlani, the sacred semen of Uluhina.

Hānau Kahoʻolawe, he lōpā.

Kahoʻolawe was born, a tenant farmer.

Kiʻina aku Uluhina

Uluhina then was called upon;

Moku ka piko o ke kamaiki,

The umbilical cord of the little one was cut,

Ka ʻiewe o ke keiki i lele

The afterbirth of the child was thrown

I komo i loko o ka ʻape nalu, ka ʻapeʻape kai ʻaleʻale,

Into the folds of the rolling surf, the froth of the heaving sea.

Loaʻa ka malo o ke kama,

Then was found the loincloth for the child.

ʻO Molokini ka moku

It is the island, Molokini,

He ʻiewe ia, ā. He ʻiewe ka moku.

That is the afterbirth, yes. The island is the afterbirth. . . .

Preceding page
Kahoʻolawe's abundant marine life first attracted Hawaiian settlers to the island, and its reefs remain among the richest in Hawaiʻi. Their good condition relative to reefs of the other main islands may result from the military's frequent closure of the island's inshore waters, which protected them from overfishing and other damage.

Across the ʻAlalākeiki channel, past the islet of Molokini, lies the great volcanic cone of Haleakalā, Maui. Several early chants and stories speak of a close relationship between Kahoʻolawe and these neighbors, Maui and Molokini.

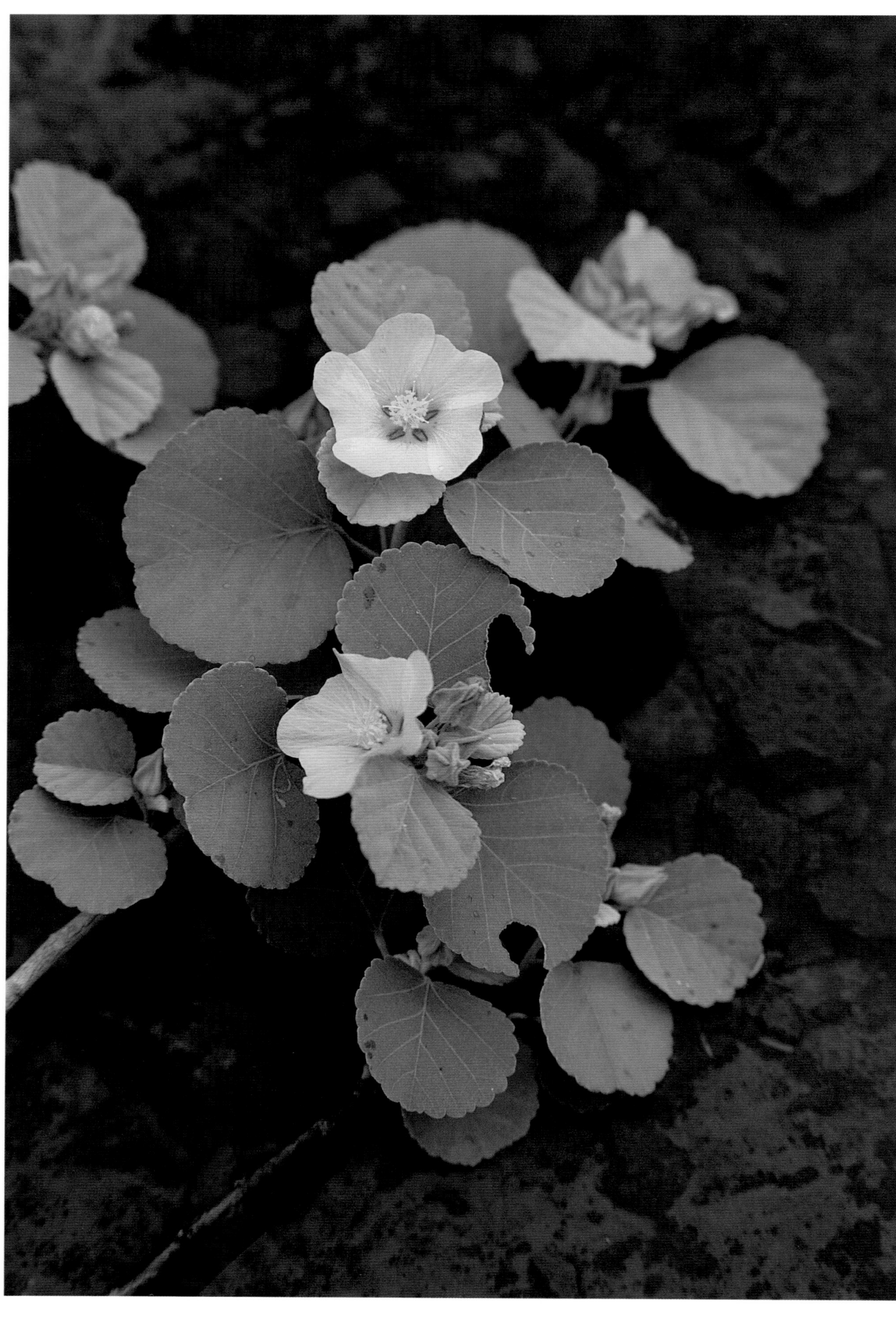

Preceding page ↩
A prominent pillar of stone known as Laeokaule stands at the northern head of the bay of Kanapou, pointing across the ʻAlalākeiki channel toward Molokini and Haleakalā. At the foot of the bay's northern cliffs is Kaluaokamohoaliʻi, a sea cave associated with the revered shark god Kamohoaliʻi.

Each winter, kona *(southern) storms bring life-giving rain to Kahoʻolawe's grasslands, turning them from gold to green. Though exotic plants have taken over much of the island's lowlands, its western end still sustains numerous native species, including this golden-blossomed* ʻilima, *the largest stands of* maʻo *(Hawaiian cotton) in Hawaiʻi, and sizable patches of* pili, *a sweet-smelling native grass favored for thatching.*

He Mele Pana no Kahoʻolawe

A PLACE-NAME CHANT FOR KAHOʻOLAWE

Hānau ʻia ka pua o ke kai, ʻo Kanaloa

The progeny of the sea, Kanaloa, was born—

Ke keiki iʻa a Papa, a Haumea, a Hina

The fish child of the female deities Papa, Haumea, and Hina,

ʻO nā mākua wahine e ulu ai

Matrons of protection

ʻO ke kai ʻo Kealaikahiki ke kākoʻo kua nō ia

The sea of Kealaikahiki is his backrest

ʻO ke kai ʻo ʻAlalākeiki ka noho no ia keiki moku

The sea of ʻAlalākeiki is the resting place of this island child

Ua hui pū ʻia ʻo Kohemālamalama iā Laeokaule

Kohemālamalama co-mingled with Laeokaule

Puka mai ʻo Kanapou

Kanapou issued forth,

Nā pali kū no ke akua Kamohoaliʻi

The upright cliffs for the god Kamohoaliʻi

Ola nō kona mau kino ma laila

Long life for his body forms there—

Aia nā manō, ʻau i ke kai

The sharks, swimming in the ocean!

Composed by the respected scholar and *kumu hula* (hula master), Pualani Kanakaʻole Kanahele, this lengthy chant celebrates some of the *wahi pana*—the noted and storied places—of the island of Kahoʻolawe. Like all traditional *mele pana* (place-name chants), it reveals something of the character, history, and lore of the places it describes. It also plays on the meanings of their names as in the line "Kohemālamalama co-mingled with Laeokaule." Kohemālamalama, one of the ancient names for Kahoʻolawe, can be translated as "bright vagina," while Laeokaule, (Lae-o-ka-ule), a prominent pillar of stone at the eastern tip of the island, means "point of the penis." After naming the channels that border Kahoʻolawe, the chant makes a circuit of the island. Beginning at the east-end bay of Kanapou, it travels down the island's spine to Kamohio, then around the west end, up the northern coast, and past Kuikui point to the bay of Hakioawa (see map on page 110). Luamakika, which the chant describes as "the highest point" on Kahoʻolawe, is a nineteenth-century name for Luamoaʻula, the volcanic crater that originally formed the island. The "Moaʻula" mentioned in the *mele* is the cindercone of Moaʻulaiki.

Pua Kanahele first offered this chant at a healing ceremony for Kahoʻolawe that was held on the island in August 1992.

During the winter rainy season, banks of low clouds occasionally settle over the peak of Moaʻulaiki, enveloping it in a soft, gray mist. This moisture feeds the lichen that mottle the rocks of the puʻu *(hill), which is the second highest point on Kahoʻolawe. On clear days, the vista across the island's central plateau extends past the low ridge of Puʻumōiwi toward the island's western end.*

Ki'eki'e ke kuahiwi 'o Luamakika

The upland of Luamakika is the highest point,

Aia ka piko o ka moku

The navel of the island

Noho ka hoa o Luamakika i kona alo

The companion of Luamakika sits in his presence

'O ia nō 'o Moa'ula

This is Moa'ula

Ha'a 'o Moa'ula i ka makani

Moa'ula dances in the breeze

Aia ka uka 'o Pu'umoiwi

The upland of Pu'umoiwi is there

Me Kealialuna lāua 'o Kealialalo

With Kealialuna and Kealialalo

'O kēia mau mea ke kualono loa no Kaho'olawe.

These are the long ridge back for Kaho'olawe

Aia iho ke awa 'o Kamohio

There below is the valley of Kamohio,

Nolu 'ehu i ka 'ehu kai

Moist with the sea spray

'Au nā nai'a i ke kai o Honokanai'a

The porpoises swim in the ocean of Honokanai'a

Ua hala aku nei i ke awāwa 'o Waikahalulu

Just past the valley of Waikahalulu

The cinder cone of Pu'u-mōiwi was the site of the second largest adze quarry in the Hawaiian Islands. Dotted about its slopes are numerous workshops like this one, where craftsmen shaped chunks of fine-grained basalt into stone adzes, the primary wood-working tools of early Hawaiians.

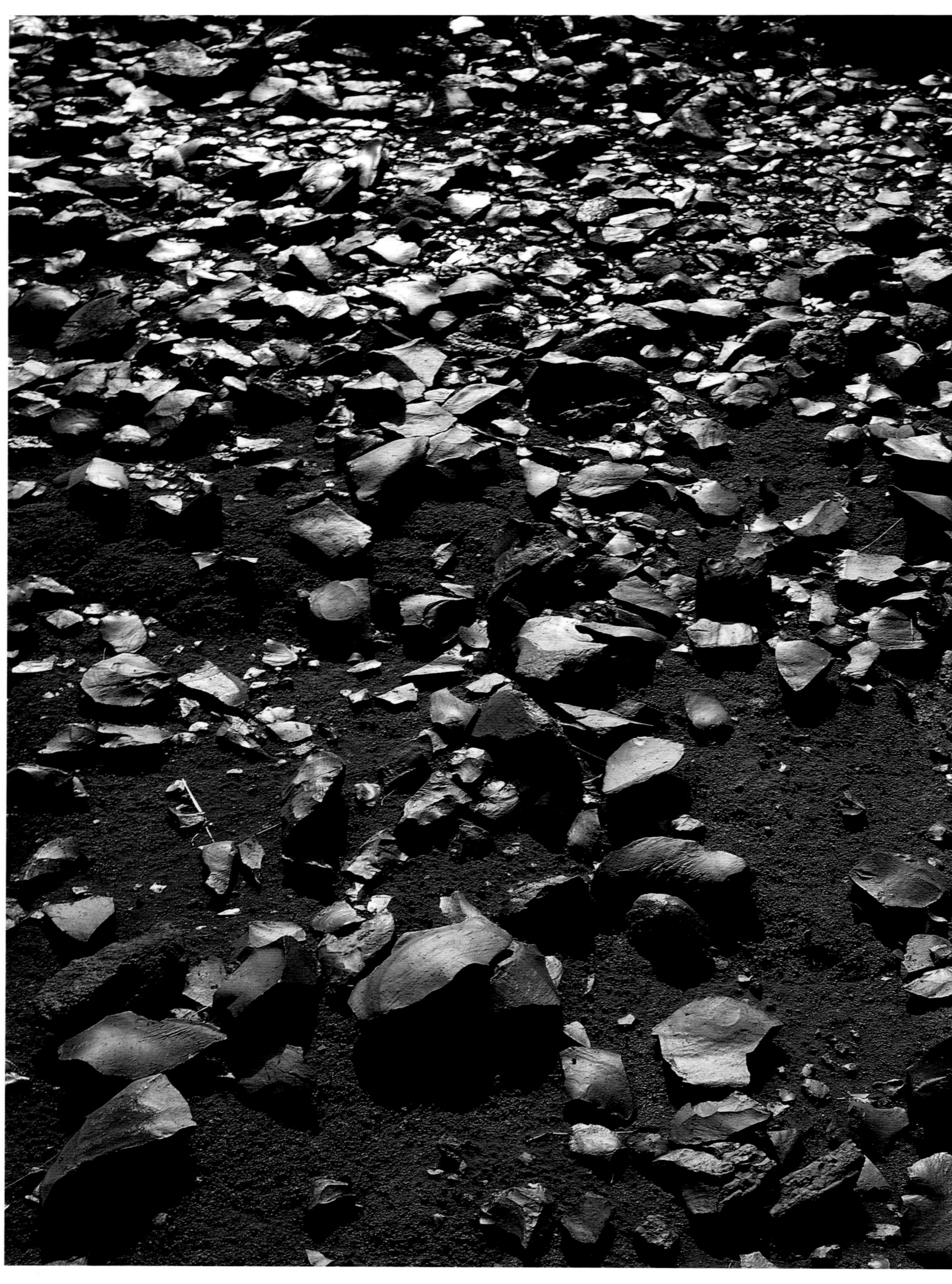

A dense scatter of basalt flakes marks the location of one of the workshops on Pu'umōiwi. Here, adze-makers used water-rounded stones to chip away at lumps of raw rock, knocking off flakes until each rock had roughly the desired shape. Unfinished adzes were then taken down to the coast to be polished and sharpened.

At each of Pu'umōiwi's adze workshops can be found a small shrine where adze-makers prayed and made offerings to their patron deities. At the largest work-shop site, a split, upright stone has been set atop a low terrace wall to form part of the shrine, while behind it a small altar platform has been erected. A number of fully shaped adzes were found in a niche below the split upright, evidently placed there as offerings.

The rocky tip of Lae-okealaikahiki reaches toward the setting sun. Early Hawaiians spoke of the west as ke alanui ma'awe 'ula a Kanaloa, *the long, much traveled path of Kanaloa.*

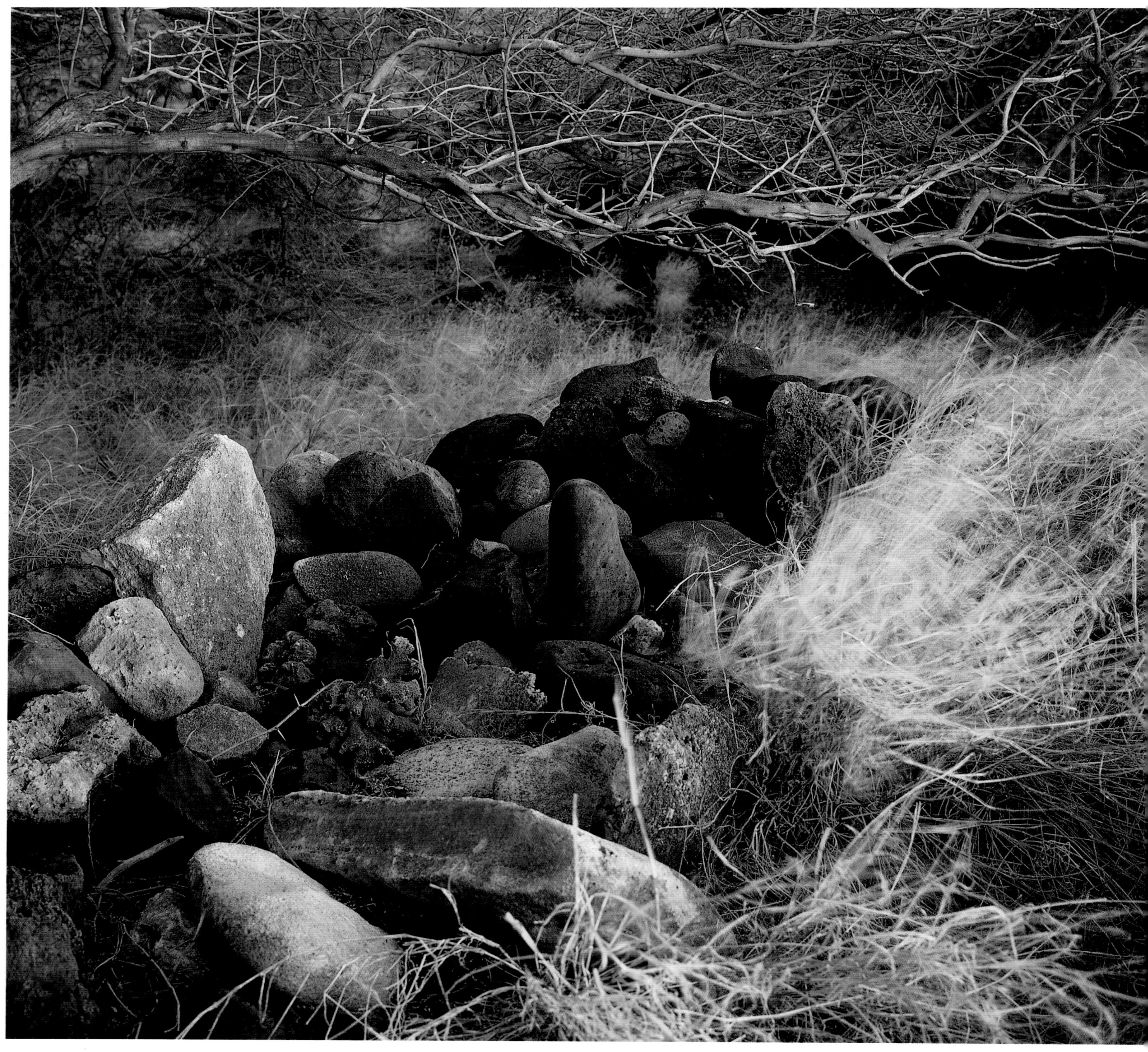

ʻO Kealaikahiki ka lae aʻe

Kealaikahiki juts out there,

Ke kuhikuhi aku nei i ke ala loa i Kahiki

Pointing out the long trail to Kahiki

He poʻo ʻoiʻoi nō ia keiki

This is a pointed-headed child

Kaulana ʻo Kuheʻia kokoke i nā māhoe

Famed Kuheʻia is close to the twins

ʻO ia hoʻi ʻo Papakaiki lāua ʻo Papakanui

Papakaiki and Papakanui

Mālamalama ke kukui o ka lae ʻo Kuikui

The light at Kuikui Point burns brightly,

E lawe mai ana i nā waʻa kaulua

Bringing the double-hulled canoes

I nā hono a Piʻilani

To the bays of Piʻilani

Ke hoʻolawe ʻia aku nei ka ʻāina ma Hakiʻoawa

The land at Hakiʻoawa is being taken

Eō mai e Hakiʻoawa

Answer, Hakiʻoawa!

E hoʻokanaloa hou iho no mākou nō, a hoʻi!

Re-establish yourself for us, and return!

This small koʻa *(fishing shrine) on Kahoʻolawe's west end is one of more than sixty that ring the island's coast. At these* koʻa, *Kahoʻolawe's fishermen laid the first of their catch as offerings of thanks to the gods.*

Following pages ⇝
The untrafficked beaches of Kahoʻolawe's west end give ample evidence of the teeming life off shore, including ula *(spiny lobster),* pū hoʻokani *(conch), and* pūpū ʻalā *(cone shells). They are also home to a small, but growing population of the endangered* ʻīlioholoikauaua *(Hawaiian monk seal).*

Preceding page ⟴
Kaho'olawe's northern coast is notched by a series of small, sheltered bays such as Kūheia, which faces across the Kealaikahiki channel toward neighboring Lāna'i. In the early years of this century, sheep and cattle raised on the island were shipped out of Kūheia by the Kaho-olawe Ranch Company.

Once home to Kaho'olawe's largest Hawaiian community, the valley of Hakioawa lies on the island's northeastern coast at the point closest to Maui. The Protect Kaho-'olawe 'Ohana, which now uses Hakioawa as its base camp, has brought some of the valley's ancient shrines back into service and has built several new structures to accommodate ceremonies, meetings, and hula.

He Mo'olelo no Molokini

AN ACCOUNT CONCERNING MOLOKINI

ʻO Molokini, he wahi moku ʻuʻuku loa ia, ʻo ia nō hoʻi kekahi heluna o nā mokupuni o Hawaiʻi nei, ua ʻane like kona nui me Kaʻula, Nihoa, Lehua, ʻo lākou nō hoʻi nā mokupuni liʻiliʻi loa o kēia pae ʻāina Hawaiʻi nei, ʻaʻole kūpono ke kanaka ke noho ma laila. ʻO ka mea hoʻi nona kēia moʻolelo, aia ʻo ia ma waena o Kahoʻolawe a me Mākena, ma Maui, aia hoʻi ma ka hikina hema mai Lahaina aku. Akā, ʻo ka mea i makemake ʻia, e ʻimi i kona kumu i loaʻa mai ai . . .

ʻO nā mākua o Molokini, ʻo Puʻuhele ka makua kāne, ʻo Puʻuokali ka makuahine, he mau moʻo kēia, aia kēlā mau puʻu e kū nei ma Kamāʻalaea ʻo ia wahi aku. I ko lāua noho ʻana, he kāne a he wahine, hāpai ihola ʻo Puʻuokali i kā lāua makahiapo, a hānau maila he kaikamahine moʻo i kū i ko lāua ʻano, a kapa ʻia aku kona inoa, ʻo Puʻuoinaina. Ua hoʻonoho ʻia ua kaikamahine nei ma Kahoʻolawe, ʻo ka inoa naʻe o Kahoʻolawe i ia manawa, ʻo Kohemālamalama; he kapu loa nō hoʻi kēlā ʻāina i ia wā, ʻaʻohe aliʻi, ʻaʻohe makaʻāinana e hele ma laila.

ʻO kekahi aliʻi hoʻi e noho ana i ia wā ma Lahaina aʻe nei, ʻo Hua, ʻo kona hānau mua, ʻo Nāmakaohua, aia ʻo ia ma Hawaiʻi i ia manawa. Akā, i ka noho ʻana o Hua a ʻono i ka manu ʻuaʻu, kēnā aku ia i nā kānaka e piʻi i kona ʻuaʻu ma uka o Olowalu, ʻaʻohe ona makemake i ka manu o kahakai; aia a loaʻa ka manu, a laila, lawe aku i ke kahuna e nānā mai i kahi i loaʻa ai ʻo kēia manu; inā e haʻi pololei mai ʻo ia e like me kā nā kānaka mea i ʻōlelo aku ai i ke aliʻi, a laila, pakele, inā ʻaʻole pololei, ʻo ka make nō ia. ʻO ka inoa o ua kahuna nei, ʻo Luahoʻomoe, a he mau keiki nō hoʻi kāna. I ka piʻi ʻana o nā kānaka, ʻaʻole i

Molokini is an islet, although it is counted as one of the Hawaiian Islands; it is comparable in size to Kaʻula, Nihoa, and Lehua, they being the smallest of this Hawaiian group, and not fit for human habitation. The subject of this story lies between Kahoʻolawe and Mākena, Maui, in a southeasterly direction from Lahaina. But what is wanted is to find out the cause of its origin. . . .

The parents of Molokini were Puʻuhele [traveling hill] the father and Puʻuokali [hill of waiting] the mother; they were lizards, those hills standing just above Māʻalaea. After they became husband and wife, Puʻuokali became pregnant with their first child, and gave birth to a daughter, a lizard like themselves, to whom was given the name Puʻuoinaina [hill of wrath]. This daughter of theirs was placed on Kahoʻolawe; the name of Kahoʻolawe at that time, however, was Kohemālamalama; it was a very kapu *[sacred or forbidden] land at that time, no chiefs or common people went there.*

There lived in Lahaina a chief named Hua, whose elder brother, Nāmakaohua, was living at Hawaiʻi. When Hua desired to get some ʻuaʻu *squabs to eat, he sent some men up to the mountains above Olowalu to get them. He had no wish for birds from the beach. When the birds were obtained, they were to be taken to the priest for him to ascertain where the birds came from; if he should give out the same information as the men had given to the chief, then he would be safe; if he should give a contrary answer, he would be killed. The name of this priest was Luahoʻomoe, and he also had children. When the men went up, they could not find any mountain birds at all, so they decided to get some shore birds. When they caught some, they daubed the feathers red with dirt so that the chief would think the birds came from the mountain. When they returned and handed the birds to the chief, he was exceedingly glad because he thought the birds came from the*

The Hawaiian text of this legend was originally set down sometime in the 1870s by Joseph K. Kahele, Jr., who was then a teenage student at the mission school of Lahainaluna. Kahele appears to have recorded the *moʻolelo* as part of a class assignment to collect folktales concerning places on and around the island of Maui. Like many Hawaiian tales, Kahele's story explains the origins of a feature on the physical landscape—in this case, the islet of Molokini—giving an account of its creation differing greatly from those in "Ea mai Hawaiʻinuiākea" and "He Moʻolelo no Māui." Kahele makes reference to a number of landmarks along the southern coast of Maui, including the bay of Māʻalaea which rests between Haleakalā and the West Maui Mountains, the hills of Puʻuhele, Puʻuokali, and Hanaʻula in the mountains of west Maui, the hill of Puʻuōlaʻi at the foot of Haleakalā, and the nearby land of Kahikinui, site of Maui's last lava flow. The tale blends a story of the *moʻo* (lizard) goddess Puʻuoinaina with the better-known legend of the priest Luahoʻomoe, and the cobbling together of these two *moʻolelo* may account for some of the narrative's disjointedness. The tale also borrows from another well-known cycle of legends, incorporating within its cast of characters the volcano goddess Pele and her lover Lohiʻau. "He Moʻolelo no Molokini" is the earliest known text to refer to Kahoʻolawe by the name Kohemālamalama. We have adapted the English translation slightly, for clarity only, not wishing to lose the schoolboy simplicity and breathlessness of the original.

loaʻa iki ka manu o uka iā lākou, manaʻo aʻela lākou e kiʻi i ka manu o kahakai; i ka loaʻa ʻana o ka manu, hamo ihola lākou i ka hulu a ʻulaʻula i ka lepo, i manaʻo aku ke aliʻi, no uka ka manu. I ka hoʻi ʻana aku o lākou a hāʻawi i ke aliʻi, ʻoliʻoli loa ihola ia, me ka manaʻo no uka ka manu. ʻŌlelo akula ua aliʻi nei i nā kānaka, e lawe i ke kahuna e nānā mai. Akā, ʻike ihola ke kahuna no kahakai ka manu, ʻōlelo akula i ke aliʻi, "ʻAʻole no uka kēia manu, no kahakai kēia manu." I ia wā, ʻōlelo aku ke aliʻi i ua kahuna nei: "ʻAʻole ʻoe e ola, ʻoiai, ua hala kāu koho ʻana; ke ʻike nei nō hoʻi au, no uka kēia manu." I ia wā, hoʻomākaukau ʻia ka imu e kālua ai i ua kahuna nei.

Ma mua naʻe o kona hoʻokomo ʻia ʻana i loko o ka imu, ʻōlelo aku ia i kāna mau keiki: "I noho ʻolua a i ʻā ka imu, a i piʻi auaneʻi ka uahi a moe i uka o Olowalu, ʻo ke ala nō ia hele ʻana, a inā e piʻi ka uahi a paʻa i kahi hoʻokahi, ʻo ko ʻolua wahi nō ia e noho ai, a laila, mai manaʻo aʻe i wahine ʻē kā ʻolua, aia kā ʻolua wahine ʻo ke kaikamahine a Puʻuhele mā, ʻo ka wahine ia, pono ka noho ʻana, ola nō hoʻi nā iwi." I ia wā nō hoʻi, hoʻokomo ʻia akula ua kahuna nei i loko o ka imu e ʻā nei, papani ʻia akula ka puka a paʻa, pouli aʻela hoʻi ka uahi, ʻeono lā o ka pouli ʻana i ka uahi, a pau ihola ka ʻā ʻana o ua imu nei. Akā, he ʻelua lā o ka noho ʻana o ua kahuna nei i loko o ka imu, a puka hou aʻela ʻo ia ma kaʻe o ka imu me ka ʻike ʻole ʻia aku; ua kuhi nō hoʻi ke aliʻi, ua make, eia kā ʻaʻole.

I ka moe ʻana hoʻi o ka uahi ma uka o Olowalu, ʻo ka hele akula nō ia o ua mau keiki nei ma laila, a hina ka uahi i luna o Hanaʻula ma laila, pōhūhū ka uahi i kahi hoʻokahi, ʻo ka piʻi nō ia o ua mau keiki nei a laila, noho.

I ia wā hoʻi, ʻo Maui nei a puni, ʻaʻohe ua, ʻaʻohe nō hoʻi he kau ao iki ma ka lewa, make nā kānaka i ka wai ʻole. ʻO ka uahi hoʻi e kau nei i luna o Hanaʻula, ua lilo aʻela i ao, a hāʻule ihola nō ka ua ma ia wahi; he mahi ʻai ka hana a ua mau keiki nei, i ʻai na ka wahine, na Puʻuoinaina.

Noho ihola hoʻi ua aliʻi nei, ʻo ia ʻo Hua, a no ka make i ka wai, pōloli nō hoʻi, holo akula ia i Hawaiʻi i kahi o kona hānau mua, a no ka nele nō hoʻi o Hawaiʻi i ka wai ʻole a me ka pōloli i ka ʻai, hoʻi maila ʻo ia a ma Wailuku. ʻAʻohe wai o Wailuku, pilikia loa ihola ka manaʻo o ua aliʻi nei, ʻo ka pili wale aʻela nō ia ma kaʻe o ka pali, a make, no laila ka mea e ʻōlelo ʻia nei, "Ahu wale nā iwi o Hua i ka lā."

I ka noho ʻana hoʻi a ua mau keiki nei a oʻo ka ʻai a lāua, kālua a moʻa, ʻo ka lawe nō ia na nā mākua hōnōai a me ka wahine. ʻO kēia mau keiki naʻe, he mau manu lāua, Kaʻakakai ka mua, ʻo Kaʻanahua ka muli. Noho maila hoʻi ka makā-

mountain. The chief told the men to take them to the priest for his inspection. The priest perceived, however, that the birds came from the seashore, so he told the chief, "These birds did not come from the mountain, these birds are from the seashore."

Then the chief said to the priest: "You shall not live, for you have guessed wrongly. I can very well see that these are mountain birds." Then and there an imu *[earth oven] was prepared in which to bake the priest.*

Before he was placed in the imu*, however, he said to his children: "You two wait until the* imu *is lighted, and when the smoke ascends, should it break for the Olowalu mountains, that indicates the path. Move along, and where the smoke becomes stationary, that indicates where you are to reside. Also, do not think of any other woman for a wife; let the daughter of Puʻuhele and his wife be your wife. With her you will live well, and your bones will be cared for. Then the priest was cast into the oven and the opening closed up tightly. The smoke arose and darkened the sky for six days before the fire in the* imu *gave out. But after the priest had been in the* imu *for two days, he reappeared and sat by the edge of the* imu *unknown to anyone, the chief thinking all the time that he was dead, but it was not so.*

When the smoke ascended and leaned towards the Olowalu mountains, the two sons went off in that direction. The cloud pointed towards Hanaʻula, and there it stood still, so the two sons ascended to the place and resided there.

Then the whole of Maui became dry; no rain, not even a cloud in the sky, and people died from lack of water. The smoke that hung over Hanaʻula became a cloud, and rain fell there. The two men [married as their father had instructed them and] became planters so as to furnish their wife Puʻuoinaina with food.

Hua, the chief, lived on, and because of the lack of water and food, he sailed for Hawaiʻi, the home of his elder brother; but because Hawaiʻi also suffered from lack of water and food he came back and lived at Wailuku. Wailuku also did not have any water, and that caused the chief to be crazed, so he stayed

Preceding page ⇜
Across the ʻAlalākeiki channel from Kahoʻolawe lie the West Maui Mountains, the setting for many of the incidents described in "He Moʻolelo no Molokini."

ula o Kauaʻi a ʻike i kēia uahi i ke kau pono i luna o Hanaʻula, holo maila ʻo ia me nā lau puaʻa ʻewalu, i mea hahau i mua o ua keiki nei, i loaʻa ke ola o kēia mau ʻāina a puni ʻo Hawaiʻi nei.

I ka hiki ʻana mai o ka makāula, e lele aku ana lāua nei i luna o nā mākua hōnōai, a hiki ka makāula i laila, lele lāua nei i Kahoʻolawe, a mai laila aʻe, hoʻi hou lāua nei i Hanaʻula, a ma laila, loaʻa i ka makāula, ʻo ia kā ka loaʻa o ka ua a hiki mai i kēia wā. I ua mau keiki nei hoʻi e noho ana i luna o Hanaʻula, me ke kau nui loa o ko lāua manaʻo iā Puʻuoinaina, kā lāua wahine, ʻaʻole hoʻi lāua i ʻike aku i ka mea a kā lāua wahine e hana nei. No ka mea, ma ia hope mai, ua kiʻi ʻo Puʻuoinaina i ke kāne a Pele, ʻo ia hoʻi ʻo Lohiʻau, ua pau akula ka manaʻo i kēlā mau kāne.

Akā, i ka lohe ʻana o Pele i kēia hana a Puʻuoinaina, lilo ihola ia i mea ʻino loa iā Pele. I ia wā ʻo ia i hoʻopuka aku ai i nā ʻōlelo ʻino loa i mua o Puʻuoinaina, a lohe ia i kēia mau ʻōlelo ʻino a Pele, ʻo ka hilahila nō ia o ua ʻo Puʻuoinaina a holo i loko o ke kai, haʻalele akula i kona ʻāina, iā Kohemālamalama, ʻo Kahoʻolawe hoʻi ka inoa i kēia wā. Noho maila hoʻi ʻo Pele i Kahikinui, a aloha i ke kāne, iā Lohiʻau, e noho ana i Keālia ma Kamāʻalaea; i ia hele ʻana mai, ua paʻa ke alanui iā Puʻuhele, ma laila ka iho ʻana a ʻau i loko o ke kai; ʻike akula naʻe ʻo ia i ka moe a kona punalua moʻo, ʻo ia hoʻi ʻo Puʻuoinaina, e moe ana mai Kahoʻolawe a hiki aku ma Mākena, ʻo ka hele maila nō ia o Pele a ʻoʻoki ihola ma waenakonu o ua moʻo nei, a kaʻawale ka hiʻu, kaʻawale ke poʻo. ʻO ka hiʻu, ʻo ia ʻo Puʻuōlaʻi ma Mākena, ʻo ke poʻo hoʻi, ʻo ia ʻo Molokini. Akā, i ka lohe ʻana o nā kāne ua make kā lāua wahine, nānā akula lāua ʻo ke kū mai o ke poʻo o kā lāua lei aloha i loko o ke kai, kapa akula lāua i ka inoa o ua wahi moku nei, ʻo Molokini. ʻO ia ihola kahi moʻolelo no kona hānau ʻia ʻana mai e kona mau mākua, i loaʻa ai kēia inoa hou ʻo Molokini.

out at the edge of the precipice until he died, and that was the origin of the saying "The bones of Hua rattle in the sun."

These sons lived until their food was ripe, then they cooked it and carried it to their parents-in-law and their wife. These sons, however, were birds; Kaʻakakai was the elder and Kaʻanahua was the younger. A prophet living at Kauaʻi noticed this smoke hanging right over Hanaʻula, so he sailed toward it with many pigs to be offered as a sacrifice to these sons, that life might be restored to the whole of the Hawaiian Islands.

When the prophet arrived, these two flew to the parents-in-law; when the prophet pursued them there, they flew to Kahoʻolawe; and from there they returned to Hanaʻula, where the prophet met them [and offered his sacrifice]; and that was how the rain was restored. While these sons lived at Hanaʻula, they thought a great deal of Puʻuoinaina, their wife, but they did not know what she was doing. Puʻuoinaina had gone after Lohiʻau, the husband of Pele, and had forgotten her own husbands.

But when Pele heard what Puʻuoinaina had done she became angry. She cursed Puʻuoinaina, and when Puʻuoinaina heard this cursing from Pele, she felt so ashamed that she ran into the sea. She left her home, Kohemālamalama, now called Kahoʻolawe. Pele, residing at Kahikinui, thought so much of her husband, Lohiʻau, who was living at Keālia, Māʻalaea, that she started out to meet him; but she found her way blocked by Puʻuhele [Puʻuoinaina's father], so she went from there and waded through the sea. She saw her lizard rival, Puʻuoinaina, stretching from Kahoʻolawe to Mākena, so she came along and cut the lizard in two, right in the middle, separating the tail from the head. The tail became Puʻuōlaʻi at Mākena, and the head became Molokini. When the husbands heard that their wife was dead, they looked and beheld the head of their beloved standing in the sea, so they called the islet Molokini [many ties]. That is the story of how it was born of its parents and how it obtained this new name Molokini.

He Mo'olelo no Māui

AN ACCOUNT OF MĀUI

I ke au kahiko loa ua hele akula ke kupua Māui me kāna makau ʻo Mānaiakalani ma ka mokupuni ʻo Kahoʻolawe. Kūkā ihola ʻo ia me nā akua, a hoʻoholo like ihola i ko lākou manaʻo e huki i ka mokupuni ʻo Kahoʻolawe a hoʻopili pū me ka mokupuni ʻo Maui. Hoʻolou ihola Māui i kāna makau i ka mokupuni ʻo Kahoʻolawe, a hoʻomaka akula lākou e huki. A ʻo ka manawa a lākou e huki nei, i ka pō nō ia. Aia lākou e huki ana, aia hoʻi ua māʻamaʻama ʻē aʻela ia manawa. ʻIke maila nā kānaka e noho ana ma Honuaʻula i kēia ʻāina e ʻoni aku ana i loko o ke kai, a hoʻomaka aʻela lākou e uā. A ʻo ia ka manawa o nā akua i huli ai a nānā i hope. A i ia wā koke nō i nahā mai ai kahi i lou ʻia ai ka makau. Aia hoʻi, ua kaʻawale maila kēlā ʻāpana o ka mokupuni ʻo Kahoʻolawe a kū ihola i loko o ke kai ma waena o Kahoʻolawe a me ka mokupuni ʻo Maui, a i kapa ʻia hoʻi i kēia manawa, ʻo Molokini. A i ka ʻike ʻana o nā akua ua pahemo mai ka makau, no ka mea he kānāwai paʻa ia, ʻo ia hoʻi, ʻaʻole huli hope i ka manawa e huki ʻia ai kekahi mea, ua hoʻomaka aʻela lākou e kūmākena. A pēlā i kapa ʻia ai kēlā awa kū moku ma Honuaʻula, Maui, ʻo Kūmākena, ma muli o ke kūmākena ʻana o nā akua. ʻO ia kahi o nā akua i pae aku ai.

In very ancient times, the demigod Māui traveled around the island of Kahoʻolawe with his hook, Mānaiakalani. He talked with the gods, and they decided to pull Kahoʻolawe and join it together with the island of Maui. So Māui connected his hook to Kahoʻolawe and they began to pull. At this time the night was dark, but while they were pulling, it prematurely became light. The people living at Honuaʻula saw this land moving along in the sea and began to clamor. The gods turned to look back, and at that point, the place where the hook was connected broke off. Then that section of the island separated from the rest of Kahoʻolawe and stood in the sea between Kahoʻolawe and Maui. It is now called Molokini. When the gods saw that the hook had come loose, though it is a firm rule not to turn back while pulling something, they began to lament. That is how the harbor at Honuaʻula came to be called Kūmākena [lament]. That is the place where the lamenting gods came ashore.

This image of a fishhook, carved over seven hundred years ago, today is visible only as a mottled shadow against the weathered skin of the boulder. The 12½-inch-long petroglyph on the slopes above Hakioawa serves as a reminder of the importance fishing held in the lives of Kahoʻolawe's early inhabitants.

This little-known legend of the demigod Māui was recorded in 1921 by Theodore Kelsey, a respected collector of Hawaiian lore. He heard it from J. P. Hale, a Hawaiian elder from Maui, who at that time was living in Hilo, on the island of Hawaiʻi. The legend provides yet another account of the creation of Molokini, again linking the islet to Kahoʻolawe, but in a quite different way from "Ea mai Hawaiʻinuiākea" and "He Moʻolelo no Molokini." Hale's tale is a variation on the well known story of how Māui and his brothers (here identified as *akua*, gods) attempted to draw together all the islands of the Hawaiian chain.

Oli Kūhohonu o Kaho'olawe mai nā Kūpuna mai

DEEP CHANT OF KAHO'OLAWE FROM OUR ANCESTORS

KĀHEA

CALL

'U'ina, kaulona i ka pū waikaua

'U'ina, listen to the conch shell

Wehewehe mai nei kahi ao

Dawn is breaking

Kū mai nā wa'a kaulua

Two double-hulled canoes are sighted

Pūē ke kanaka mai ka wa'a mai

The men cheer from the canoe

Kūkulu ka iwi o ka 'āina, 'Ailana Kohemalamalama

Land is sighted, to your left it is like heaven all lit up

Ho'ohiki kēia moku iā Kanaloa

We dedicate this island to Kanaloa

Akua o ka moana 'ili, moana uli

God of the shallow and deep ocean

Ke holo nei me ke au kāhili

We are running in an erratic current

'Ōhaehae mai ka makani

The wind is blowing from all directions

'Alalā keiki pua ali'i

The chief's child is crying

Ka piko hole pelu o Kanaloa

The curled navel of Kanaloa

The late Harry Kūnihi Mitchell recorded the words of this *mele* from memory in the early 1980s and published them in the Hawaiian-language newspaper *Ka Makani Kahaukāne.* He prefaced the chant by stating that "Here written below is an ancient chant pertaining to the island of Kaho'olawe. I heard this chant from the lips of my ancestors in the days of my youth. This is an old chant from the beginning of creation." Mitchell elsewhere explained that he had learned the chant from his grandmother's cousin, Kealoha Kū'ike, and that he had worked for many years to perfect his recollection and translation of it. In his introduction to the chant, Mitchell also noted that its verses contain "the names of Kaho'olawe, from the beginning of time" and listed them, with possible translations, as follows:

1. *Kohemalamalama*
   To your left and lit up
2. *Kanaloa*
   One of the four major gods
3. *Hineli'i* Light rain
4. *Kahikimoe* Where the sun sets
5. *Kaho'olawe*
   To take and to embrace

The tenth through twelfth lines of the *mele* involve a play on 'Alalākeiki, the name of the channel that lies between Kaho'olawe and Maui and encloses the islet of Molokini, the "curled navel of Kanaloa."

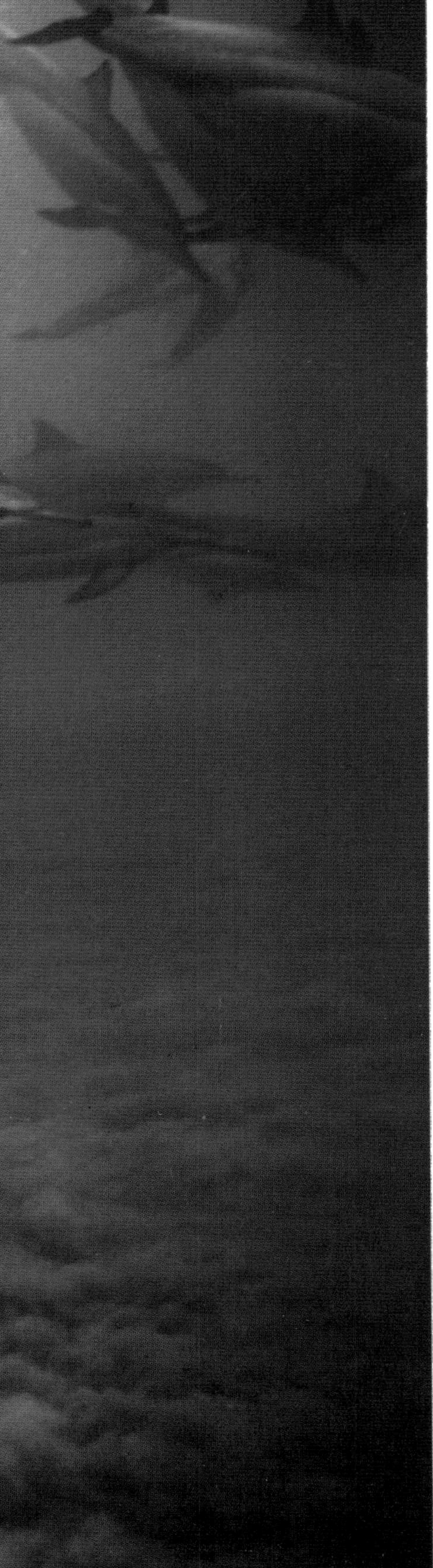

Kahua pae ʻili kīhonua āhua

The channel is shallow

Puehu ka lepo o Moaʻula

Dust is spreading over Mount Moaʻula

Puʻuhonua moʻo kahuna kilo pae honua

Gathering place of the kahuna *classes to study astronomy*

Pōhaku ahu ʻaikūpele kāpili o Keaweiki

Stone of deep magic of Keaweiki

Kau lī lua ka makani ke hae nei

The wind that tears along is chilly

Kāwele hele nei ʻo Heneliʻi, nāpoʻo ka lā i Kahikimoe

Light rain is falling, the sun is setting towards Kahikimoe

Nue mai ke ao Lanikau

The glow after the sunset is like the colors of the rainbow

Kapu mai ka honua, kūpaʻa loa

The world seems to be standing still

Pau ka luhi ʻana o ka moana

We shall no more labor on the ocean

Manaʻo hālana pū i ke Akua

My thoughts are enlightened towards God

He aloha pili kau no kēia ʻāina

My love for this land will always be deep within my heart

Aloha nō ka mana o nā kūpuna

I love the knowledge and power of my ancestors

Preceding page
At the peak of Moaʻulaiki rests the stone slab referred to in Harry Mitchell's chant as the "stone of deep magic of Keaweiki." Its location provides a perfect vantage point from which to view the neighboring islands—here Lānaʻi and Molokaʻi—as well as to study the movement of the winds, the currents, and the stars. These were important guides to the early Hawaiian navigator, making it readily understandable why Moaʻulaiki came to be a "gathering place of the kahuna *classes to study astronomy."*

Nā Wai Puna o Kamohio no Kahoʻolawe

THE SPRING WATERS OF KAMOHIO ON KAHOʻOLAWE

Kahoʻolawe's southern cliffs extend in an unbroken palisade from the eastern headland of Hanakanaiʻa, past the deep-cut bays of Waikahalulu and Kamohio, to Laeokākā at the eastern end of the island. Along this southern coast, botanists recently discovered a previously unknown plant, which has since been given the name Kapalupaluokanaloa (the gentleness of Kanaloa). Pollen studies show that this low shrub was once common in dry areas of Oʻahu and other Hawaiian islands, but it now survives only on the sea-stack of ʻAleʻale, where it has been protected by driving surf and 600 feet of near-vertical rock.

ʻUʻina Haʻi

Revelation

Mai ke kumu o Lanikau

From the source from heaven above

Ka maka o Lonokaʻehokūānuenue

The eyes of the god Lonokaʻeho-who-stands-on-the-rainbow

E pili i ke kumu o Kahiki

Whose knowledge comes from the creation of Kahiki

Ke kumu o Moaʻulanuiākea i hānau ʻia

Born from the kahuna *class of Moaʻulanuiākea*

Kumu uli paʻa o nā kūpuna

With deep knowledge of his ancestors' teachings

Mai ke kihi o ka hono ʻo Kamohio i hikina

And from the east bend of Kamohio Bay

Ka wai puna pua o Kāne

Spring forth the flower waters of Kāne

Me ka wai heʻe o Kanaloa

And the slippery waters of Kanaloa

Nā wai wili lua ke kau nei

Which are hidden high in the cliffs

Kau lī lua i ka puʻu ke ʻapu iho

They are cool and refreshing to drink

Like the "Oli Kūhohonu o Kahoʻolawe mai nā Kūpuna mai," this mele was passed down to Harry Kūnihi Mitchell by his grandmother's cousin. Mitchell recorded the chant as he remembered it and produced his own translation. In a brief introduction to the chant Mitchell explained, "I am revealing the story I heard from my *kupuna* [ancestor] Kealoha Kūʻike about the priest Kahuna Kamohio and of his knowledge of his ancestor's teaching of creation and of the spring waters on the east end of Kamohio Bay on Kahoʻolawe." Kamohio is a narrow, cliff-rimmed bay on the island's southern coast. The spring described in the chant appears to lie high in the cliffs, where water seeps from layers of lava. A knowledge of the location of such water sources was vital to the survival of Kahoʻolawe's early inhabitants.

Nihi pali ke alo o nā wai

The trail leading to the springs is dangerous to traverse

Kūmanamana ka pōhaku kau pueo ʻula

The pillar rock above is like a red owl

Mai ke alo o Wākea hoʻohaulani moku i ʻō

The presence of the god Wākea towards the land brings good feelings

Kū haʻililani kapu ʻo Kanaloa—Kahoʻolawe

The heavens declare the kapu *on Kanaloa—Kahoʻolawe*

ʻUlalena ka ua ke nihi nei

The reddish rain is creeping over the land

Kukū ka ʻale o ka makani

The wind is stirring up white caps

Hololua, holopili, holokake

The wind is blowing from three directions

Kuakea ka ʻili o ka honua

The ocean is covered with white caps

Mōlehulehu ke alo o ka honua

It's beginning to get dark over the land

Hele nahe ka hōkū ke kau nei

The evening star is slowly appearing

Mai komohana, kūkulu hema, kūkulu ʻākau, hikina

Followed by stars from West, South, North, and East

Naue mai ke aloha no ka ʻāina Kanaloa—Kahoʻolawe

I love this island of Kanaloa—Kahoʻolawe

During a 1913 expedition to Kahoʻolawe, archaeologist John F. G. Stokes discovered in the bay of Kamohio a shrine consisting of a shelter cave and five stone-edged terraces extending up the adjoining talus slope. Atop these terraces, half buried in layers of pili *and fern, Stokes found numerous offerings, upright stones, and a carved wooden image, wrapped to its forehead in* kapa *(bark cloth). Stokes spent several weeks excavating the shrine and removed most of its artifacts, which are now in the collections of the Bernice Pauahi Bishop Museum. Some time after Stokes finished his work, a rockfall completely buried the terraces, and in 1990, only months after the military stopped its bombing of Kahoʻolawe, the cave itself was looted for artifacts.*

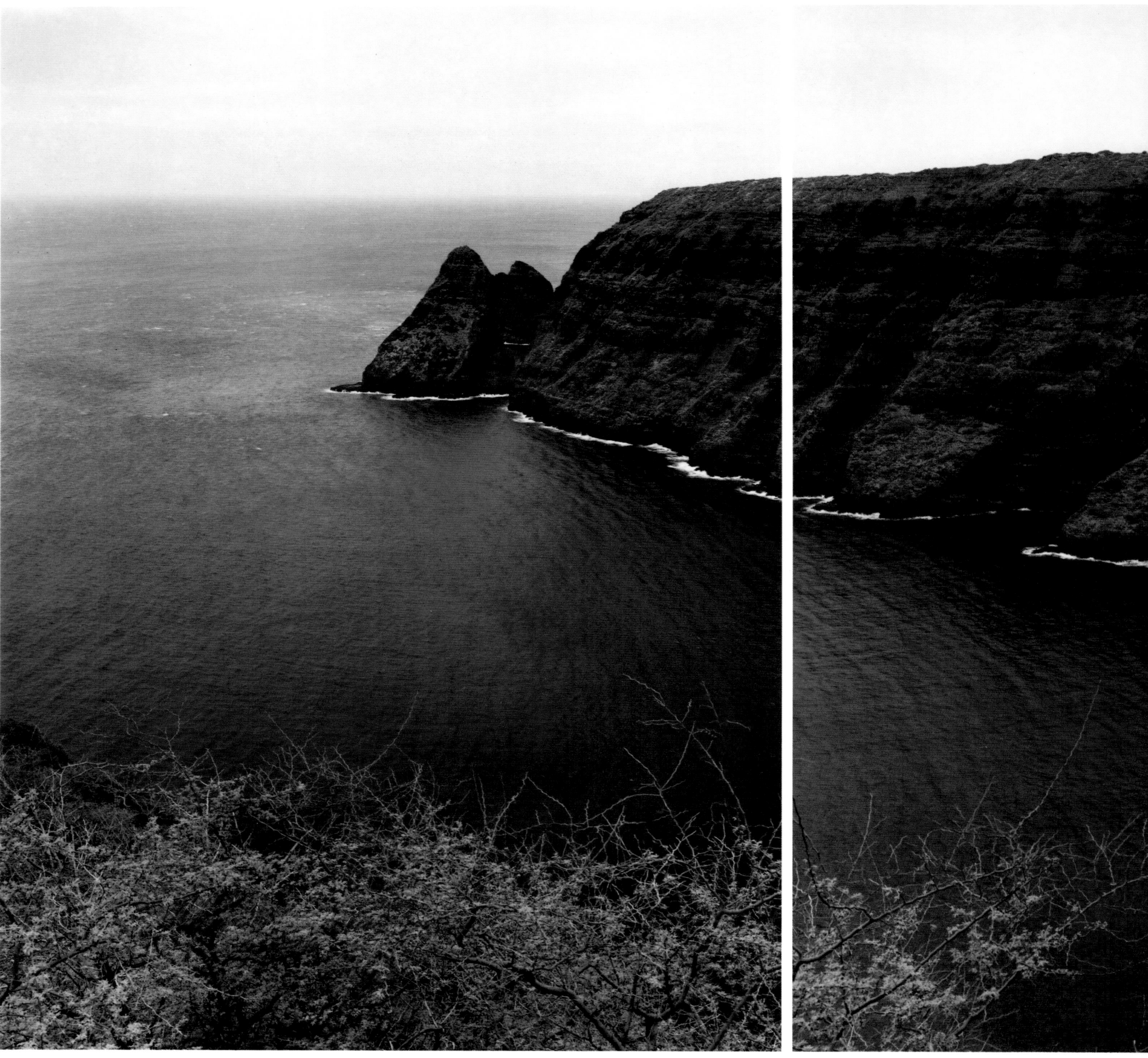

Ka'ao no Kalaepuni

LEGEND OF KALAEPUNI

ʻO Kalanipō ka makua kāne, ʻo Kamaʻelekapu ka wahine, ʻo Kalaepuni ka mua, ʻo Kalaehina ka muli, a ʻo Hōlualoa i Kona, Hawaiʻi, ka ʻāina; ʻo Keaweanuia-ʻumi ke aliʻi o Hawaiʻi i ia wā e noho ana. No Kalaepuni. He keiki kolohe loa ia a me ka makaʻu ʻole, ʻeono ona mau makahiki, hoʻomaka ʻo ia e pepehi i kona poʻe hoa pāʻani; mai laila ka piʻi ʻana o kona ikaika a hiki i ka iwakālua o kona mau makahiki. Lilo aʻela ʻo Kalaepuni i mea kaulana ma Hawaiʻi a puni, manaʻo ihola ia e pepehi i nā keiki aliʻi a pau loa o Hawaiʻi, mai ka mea nunui a ka mea liʻiliʻi loa, a ka mea e omo ana i ka waiū. A ʻo Keawenuiaʻumi hoʻi, ʻaʻole ona manaʻo e pepehi, no ka mea ua kokoke mai kona wā ʻelemakule; no laila, waiho kona manaʻo iā Keawenuiaʻumi. Akā, ua komo ka makaʻu o Keawenuiaʻumi iā Kalaepuni, a manaʻo ihola e mahuka mai nā maka aku o Kalaepuni.

Ma hope o laila, holo akula ʻo Kalaepuni me nā lawaiʻa a Keawenuiaʻumi ma waho aʻe o Kalāhiki, he kūpalupalu manō kā lākou lawaiʻa. A mākaukau nā manō a pau loa ma lalo o nā waʻa o lākou, huki nā lawaiʻa a Keawenuiaʻumi i ka manō i luna o nā waʻa, lele ihola ʻo Kalaepuni i waena o nā manō a pepehi ihola i nā manō i laka mai me ke kūpalu ʻana, a lanakila ʻo Kalaepuni ma luna o nā manō a pau loa. A laila, ʻōlelo iho ʻo Kalaepuni i kāna ʻōlelo kaena penei: "Ma kēia hope aku, e hoʻolilo ana wau i oʻu mau lima i makau kīhele manō! A

Kalanipō and Kamaʻelekapu were the father and mother of Kalaepuni and Kalaehina. Kalaepuni was the elder and Kalaehina the younger. They were born and raised in Hōlualoa, Kona, during the reign of Keawenuiaʻumi, king of Hawaiʻi. Kalaepuni was a very mischievous boy who was without fear. At the age of six he was able to whip all his playmates, and his strength developed from that time on until he reached the age of twenty, at which time Kalaepuni became famous over the whole of Hawaiʻi for his great strength. At twenty he determined to strike down all the young chiefs of Hawaiʻi, those who were of very high birth as well as those of low birth, both big and small, even those still at the breast. In his plan to strike down all the chiefs, he did not intend to include Keawenuiaʻumi because, he reasoned, Keawenuiaʻumi was already well advanced in years. But Keawenuiaʻumi was afraid of Kalaepuni, and he made plans to escape and get out of Kalaepuni's presence.

Shortly after the events narrated above, Kalaepuni went out with some of Keawenuiaʻumi's fishermen to the fishing grounds outside of Kalāhiki; they went out shark fishing. After some of the bait was thrown out, the sharks began to gather under the canoe, and when the baited hooks were let down, several sharks were caught and hauled into the canoe. While Keawenuiaʻumi's men were hauling in the sharks, Kalaepuni jumped out among the other sharks that had gathered under the canoe and began to fight them, killing them all. After killing all the sharks, Kalaepuni began boasting, saying: "Henceforth I shall use my hands as hooks for

---

This story, which recounts the life and death of the *kupua* (demigod) Kalaepuni, was one of many *moʻolelo* collected in the late 1800s by Abraham Fornander, and subsequently published in the *Fornander Collection of Hawaiian Antiquities and Folk-lore.* The legend is set in the time of Keawenuiaʻumi, son of the great chief ʻUmi and *aliʻi nui* (paramount chief) of the island of Hawaiʻi. While much of the tale takes place on Hawaiʻi, where Kalaepuni was born and grew to manhood, its climax occurs at a bay on the eastern coast of Kahoʻolawe, here called "Keanapou." This appears to have been the old name of the bay and to have been shortened over time to Kanapou. The legend's description of the well at Kanapou as "ten fathoms in depth" seems exaggerated. Hawaiian wells were not deeply excavated shafts but shallow pits dug to improve a natural spring or seep. A more accurate description of this well, by someone who actually drank from it, can be found in "Ka Lawaiʻa ʻOpihi." Sharks, another element central to the Kalaepuni legend, play a recurring role in traditions related to Kahoʻolawe, including "He Moʻolelo Kaʻao no Kaʻehuikimanōopuʻuloa" and "Ka Lawaiʻa ʻOpihi." In his book *Ruling Chiefs of Hawaii,* Samuel Kamakau mentions a historic Kalaepuni, a warrior in the court of ʻUmi who was skilled at capturing and killing sharks.

This petroglyph is one of several lively human figures hewn into a cluster of boulders on the upper slopes of Moaʻulanui. Archaeologists have suggested that these figures may represent runners or perhaps dancers.

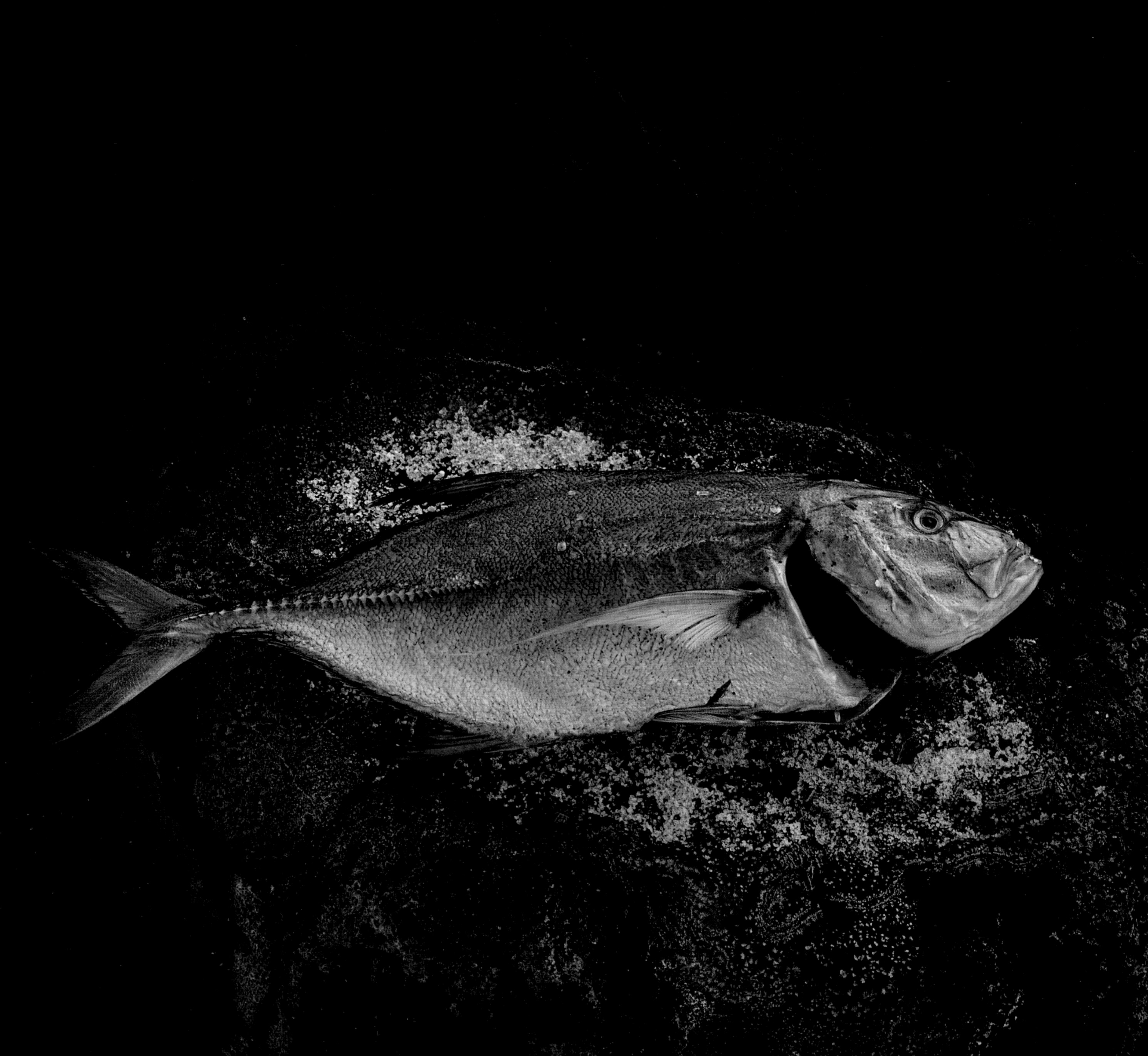

catching sharks and shall make all sharks dust in my hands."

After they had been fishing for some time, they returned and landed their canoe at Hōnaunau where a large kou *tree was standing. This was a very large tree, requiring three men [holding hands] to span its girth. Kalaepuni, however, took hold of the tree and pulled it up by the roots, as though it was but a blade of grass, so unresisting was it. After pulling up the tree, he again boasted, saying: "I am going to turn my hands into an axe to cut down trees for canoes in Hilo."*

Because of these feats of strength that Kalaepuni accomplished before the king, Keawenuiaʻumi became more and more afraid, and he hid in a place behind the mountain of Hualālai, between Maunaloa and the Kona mountain. The place became famous after this because it was here that Keawenuiaʻumi lived in hiding, at Ahuaʻumi, which can be seen to this day, lying behind the Kona mountain in the eastern part of that district.

Before Keawenuiaʻumi went off to hide, he left word with one of his servants, Maunaloa, as follows: "I am now on my way. If Kalaepuni comes while you are here, tell him that I am dead." The servant consented. Keawenuiaʻumi then departed to the place mentioned above. After his departure, Kalaepuni arrived at the house and asked Maunaloa the king's whereabouts. Maunaloa answered that the king was dead. Kalaepuni then took charge of the whole island of Hawaiʻi, reigning as king in place of Keawenuiaʻumi.

While Keawenuiaʻumi was hiding, one day he said to his high priest, Mokupane: "You must invoke the gods for the death of Kalaepuni so that I may again reign as king of the whole of Hawaiʻi." Soon after the king made this request, Mokupane the priest went to Kahoʻolawe by canoe with eighty men, directing them to dig a well ten fathoms in depth and to place large rocks around its mouth. The name of the land where

e hoʻolilo au i nā manō a pau i lehu i loko o kuʻu poho lima."

A pau ka lawaiʻa ʻana, hoʻi akula lākou a pae ka waʻa ma Hōnaunau, e kū ana he kumu kou nui i laila; ʻo ka nui o ua kou lā, ʻekolu kānaka e apo me nā lima, a laila, puni kona kino. Lālau ihola ʻo Kalaepuni i ke kumu kou a huhuki aʻela, ua like me ka mauʻu ʻōpala iā ia, ka māunu a uaua ʻole ke huhuki aʻe. A laila, waiho ihola ia i kāna ʻōlelo kaena, penei: "E hoʻolilo ana au i oʻu mau lima i koʻi kua waʻa no Hilo."

A no kēia mau mea a Kalaepuni i hōʻike ai i mua o ke aliʻi, o Keawenuiaʻumi, makaʻu ihola ʻo Keawenuiaʻumi, a mahuka akula a noho ma ke kua o ka mauna ʻo Hualālai, ma waena o Maunaloa a me ka mauna o Kona. Ua kaulana ia wahi i noho ʻia e Keawenuiaʻumi,ʻo ia ʻo Ahuaʻumi a hiki i kēia lā, e waiho lā ma ka mauna o Kona, ma ka hikini o Kona.

Ma mua aʻe o ka mahuka ʻana o Keawenuiaʻumi, waiho ihola ia i kāna ʻōlelo i kekahi kauā āna, iā Maunaloa: "Eia wau ke hele nei, i noho ʻoe i hiki mai ʻo Kalaepuni, ʻōlelo aku ʻoe, ua make au." ʻAe akula ke kauā, hele akula ʻo Keawenuiaʻumi a noho i kahi i ʻōlelo mua ʻia ma luna aʻe nei. A hele ʻo Keawenuiaʻumi, hiki ʻo Kalaepuni a ka hale, nīnau iā Maunaloa, ʻōlelo mai ʻo Maunaloa: "Ua make." A laila, lawe aʻela ʻo Kalaepuni iā Hawaiʻi i loko o kona lima, a lilo ihola ko Keawenuiaʻumi noho ʻana aliʻi iā ia.

Iā Keawenuiaʻumi e noho ana i ka mauna, ʻōlelo akula ia i kāna kahuna, iā Mokupane: "E ʻanāʻanā ʻoe iā Kalaepuni a make, i lilo hou au i aliʻi no Hawaiʻi a puni." Ma hope o kēia ʻōlelo a ke aliʻi i ke kahuna, hoʻouna akula ʻo Mokupane i ʻelua kanahā kanaka i Kahoʻolawe, ma luna o nā waʻa, e kōhi i pūnāwai, he ʻumi anana ka hohonu, a e hoʻopuni ʻo luna i nā pōhaku nunui loa. ʻO ka ʻāina i kōhi ʻia ai ka pūnāwai, ʻo Keanapou [Kanapou] i Kahoʻolawe, aia nō ke waiho lā a hiki i kēia lā, hoʻonoho ʻia ihola he ʻelemakule me kāna wahine i ua pūnāwai nei, he mau lawaiʻa lāua.

A mākaukau ka hoʻi o nā kanahā kānaka ʻelua i Hawaiʻi, ʻōlelo aku ʻo Mokupane, ke kahuna, i nā ʻelemākule: "Ē, i noho ʻolua a i hiki mai he kanaka nui, ua ʻākī ʻia ka lauoho, ua like ka lōʻihi me ka pū o ke olonā, a laila, ʻo ke kanaka ia nona kēia pūnāwai, a ma ʻane'i ʻo ia e make ai. A hiki mai iō ʻolua nei, hāʻawi aku ʻolua i ka iʻa a pau loa iā ia, nāna ia e ʻai a make i ka wai, a i noi mai iā ʻolua i wai, mai hāʻawi ʻolua i ka wai, kuhikuhi aku ʻolua i ka wai i ka luawai nei lā." Ma hope o kēia ʻōlelo ʻana a ke kahuna, hoʻi akula lākou a hiki i Hawaiʻi, i ia wā, hoʻomaka ʻo Mokupane i kāna pule ʻanāʻanā no Kalaepuni. Ma hope o kēia pule ʻana a Mokupane, ua kuʻi aʻela ke kaulana o ke kū ʻana o ka manō ma Kauhola i Kohala, ma nā wahi o Hawaiʻi a puni, a lohe ʻo Kalaepuni, kupu aʻela kona manaʻo e hele e leʻaleʻa me ka manō ma Kauhola, no ka mea, ua ʻōlelo ʻia, ʻo kāna puni ka hakakā me ka manō.

A hiki ia i Kohala, a hehi i luna o Kauhola, e paʻapū ana nā kānaka i laila, e nānā ana i ka manō; i ia wā, lele ʻo Kalaepuni i lalo a hakakā me ka manō; nui nā manō i make iā ia ma kēia hakakā ʻana. No ka nanea loa o Kalaepuni i ka hakakā me ka manō, ua ʻike ʻole ia i ke kō a ke au i ʻAlenuihāhā; ʻekolu pō, ʻekolu ao i ka moana, pae i Keanapou i Kahoʻolawe, nānā akula ia, he wahi hale e kū ana, hele akula ia a hiki i laila. Nānā akula ʻo Kalaepuni, he ʻelemakule a he luahine e noho ana, aloha maila lāua, aloha akula ʻo Kalaepuni, nīnau mai lāua: "Ma ka moana mai nei ʻoe?"

ʻAe aku ʻo Kalaepuni: "ʻAe, ʻekolu pō, ʻekolu ao, hiki maila au i ʻaneʻi." ʻĪ aku ʻo Kalaepuni, "ʻAʻohe ʻai a ʻolua?"

Hōʻole mai lāua: "ʻAʻohe ʻai o kēia wahi, aia ko ʻoneʻi ʻai i ka ihu o ka waʻa, inā e holo mai ka waʻa mai Honuaʻula mai, a mai Ukumehame mai, a laila ola kēia wahi. He ʻai nō ko ʻoneʻi, i ka ʻai kamaʻāina nō, ʻo ke kūpala."

ʻAlawa aʻela ʻo Kalaepuni i luna, a ʻike i nā haka iʻa e kaulaʻi ana, nīnau akula: "Na wai kēlā iʻa?"

"Na māua nō," wahi a nā ʻelemākule.

Nonoi akula ʻo Kalaepuni iā lāua: "Naʻu kekahi iʻa." ʻAe maila lāua, noke aku ana ʻo Kalaepuni i ka ʻai i ka iʻa, a pau iā ia. Nīnau hou ʻo Kalaepuni: "Pau maila nō ka iʻa?"

ʻĪ aku lāua nei: "ʻElua ipu iʻa maka i koe, ua liʻu i ka paʻakai." Lālau akula nō ʻo Kalaepuni, a noke akula a pau ia mau ipu iʼa. I ia wā, make wai ʻo Kalaepuni, nonoi aku i wai i nā ʻelemākule, hōʻole mai nā ʻelemākule: "ʻAʻohe o māua wai, hoʻokahi nō wai o kēia wahi, ʻo ka wai kai. A ʻo ka wai maoli, aia a ua ka ua Nāulu, a laila, loaʻa ko ʻoneʻi wai maoli, a ʻo ka wai kai, ʻo ia ko ʻoneʻi wai mau, i ʻeli ʻia i loko o ka lua." Ma hope o kēia kamaʻilio ʻana, hele akula Kalaepuni a iho i lalo o ka pūnāwai i ʻeli ʻia ai, e inu wai.

A inu ʻo Kalaepuni i ka wai i lalo o ka lua, ʻolokaʻa akula nā ʻelemākule i ka pōhaku nui, a paʻa ke kua o Kalaepuni, ʻoni aʻela nō, lele ka pōhaku, ʻolokaʻa nō lāua nei i ka pōhaku a kokoke e piha ka lua, ʻoala aʻela nō ʻo Kalaepuni, lele liʻiliʻi ka pōhaku. Ma kēia ʻolokaʻa ʻana i ka pōhaku, ʻaʻole i make ʻo Kalaepuni,

they dug the well is Keanapou and the well is there to this day. After it had been dug and the rocks set in place, an old fisherman and his wife were put in charge of it.

Before the eighty men returned to Hawaiʻi, Mokupane instructed the old couple, saying: "If a very large man with locks of hair as long as a bunch of olonā should come while you two are here, that is the man for whom this well has been prepared, and here he must die. When he comes, give him all your fish so that after he has eaten the fish he will be very thirsty. When he asks you for some water, don't give him any, but direct him to this well." After these instructions were imparted by the priest, he and the men returned to Hawaiʻi, where the priest began to invoke the gods for Kalaepuni's death.

Soon after Mokupane began his prayers, it was reported all over Hawaiʻi that great schools of sharks were being seen daily at Kauhola, off the coast of Kohala. When this was reported to Kalaepuni, he at once entertained a strong desire to go to Kauhola and have some sport with the sharks, as it was his chief delight to kill them.

When Kalaepuni arrived at Kohala and set foot at Kauhola, he saw a large number of people gathered there, looking at the sharks. When Kalaepuni saw them, he jumped in and began to fight the sharks, killing a good many of them. While Kalaepuni was busily engaged in the fight, he did not notice that he was being carried away from land by a strong current into the ʻAlenuihāhā channel. After three nights and three days in the sea, he landed at Keanapou on Kahoʻolawe. When he reached the shore, he looked about him and saw a small house nearby, to which he went. There he saw an aged couple, who greeted him. This greeting he returned, and the old people asked: "Did you come from the sea?"

Yes, said Kalaepuni. "I spent three days and nights in the sea before I landed here." Kalaepuni then asked: "Have you any food?"

The old people said: "No, there is no food in this place. The only food that you can get here is what is brought in canoes. When anyone comes from Honuaʻula or Ukumehame,

ʻaʻole i paʻa ʻia nā pōhaku, akā, ʻaʻole ia i kena i ka wai no ka paʻa ʻē o ka wai i nā pōhaku.

Ma kēia hana a nā ʻelemākule iā Kalaepuni, ʻōlelo aku ʻo Kalaepuni: "E make ana ʻolua iaʻu. ʻOni aʻela ʻo Kalaepuni mai loko aʻe o nā pōhaku paʻakikī, a hemo aʻela; ʻike nā ʻelemākule, e make ana lāua iā Kalaepuni ke piʻi aʻe i luna, no laila, holo akula ka ʻelemakule kāne. Kāhea aku ka wahine: "ʻO ka holo kā kāu, kainō ʻo ka hoʻomanawanui aʻe a make ka ʻenemi, a laila, pono, a holo aku ʻoe, pakele; e holo nō, a e make nō, e noho nō a e make nō; ʻo ka ikaika auaneʻi kēia e pakele ai ke holo aku." Ma kēia ʻōlelo a ka wahine, ʻaʻohe hoʻolohe mai o ke kāne; ʻo ka holo loa, ʻaʻohe maliu mai i ka ʻōlelo a ka wahine, akā, hoʻomanawanui nō ka wahine i ke kiola ʻana i ka pōhaku, pā ihola ka lae o Kalaepuni i ka pōhaku, a make ihola.

then we get food. The only food that grows here is kūpala *[a wild morning glory whose roots were eaten only during food shortages]."*

Kalaepuni then looked up and saw a shelf on which some fish were drying, and asked: "Who owns those fish?"

"They're ours," said the old couple.

Kalaepuni asked, "May I have some?"

The old people gave him all the fish, and Kalaepuni ate until he had finished the whole lot. Kalaepuni then asked: "Is that all the fish you have?"

The old people said: "We have two calabashes of pickled ones left." Kalaepuni took the fish from the calabashes and devoured them all. After this Kalaepuni became very thirsty and asked the old people for some water. The aged couple then said: "We have no water. The only water here is brackish. Fresh water can only be had after a rain storm; but brackish water is in a well." After this Kalaepuni went and climbed down the well to take a drink.

While Kalaepuni was drinking, the old people began to roll rocks down from around the mouth of the well. When Kalaepuni's back was covered with rocks, he would move and the rocks would roll off. The two kept on rolling rocks down until the well was almost full—without killing Kalaepuni. Kalaepuni just kept on drinking, but since the water was covered over with rocks, he could get very little.

When Kalaepuni saw that the two were intent on killing him, he called out: "I am going to kill you two!" He began to turn and twist until he had freed himself from the rocks. When the old people saw that they would be killed if Kalaepuni got to the top, the old man ran away. When the old woman saw this, she called out: "Are you going to run away? Is it not best to continue the fight until the enemy is killed? Do you suppose you can save yourself by running? You will be killed if you run and you will be killed if you stay, for with this great strength, none will ever escape!" Yet the old man kept on running and never once turned back. The old woman, however, kept on rolling rocks down till one happened to strike Kalaepuni on the head, killing him.

He Mo'olelo Ka'ao no Ka'ehuikimanōopu'uloa

A LEGENDARY TALE OF KA'EHUIKIMANŌOPU'ULOA

Moe lākou nei a ao a'e, 'o ka mākaukau ihola nō ia o ka pā'ina. A pau ia, 'o ko lākou nei holo pololei akula nō ia a hiki ana i Kaho'olawe, kahi ho'i o ke akua o ka moana, 'o Kamohoali'i ka inoa. Hālāwai akula lākou nei me ke kia'i o waho mai, nīnau akula lākou nei, "E noho ana nō anei ka 'elemakule i kona wahi?"

"'Ae," wahi a ke kia'i.

'Ōlelo akula 'o Ka'ehuikimanōopu'uloa i ke kia'i, "E hele 'oe a ha'i aku i ku'u Haku Akua, eia au 'o Ka'ehuikimanōopu'uloa, 'o ke keiki a Kapukapu mā lāua 'o Hōlei. 'O kia'i pali au o Pānau i Puna, a me nā ali'i a pau o Hawai'i, nā kauā lepo āna i kipa maila e 'ike iā ia. A e ha'i aku nō ho'i i ke 'ano o kā mākou huaka'i i hiki mai i mua o kona alo ali'i."

Hele akula ke kia'i a hiki i kahi o Kamohoali'i, ha'i akula e like me nā mea i 'ōlelo 'ia aku ai iā ia, a pane maila ke ali'i, "E ki'i aku iā lākou a ho'okipa mai." Ki'i 'ia maila lākou nei e kekahi manō ali'i 'o Ka'alamikihau ka inoa, 'o ko Honua'ula manō ali'i ia. Alaka'i 'ia akula ma loko o kekahi lua nui maika'i e pili pū ana me ko ke ali'i lua e noho ana. A komo lākou nei a pau, ho'omākaukau nā mea 'ai ma ko Ka'alamikihau lawelawe 'ana. 'Ai lākou nei; a pau ka 'ai 'ana, luana ihola ka pō. I ia manawa, ha'i maila ka 'elele a ke ali'i, "E hiki mai ana ka 'elemakule e 'ike iā 'oukou." I ia wā nō, komo mai ana 'o Kamohoali'i; ua hele a ulu ka limu a me ke ko'a i luna. Aloha pākahi maila iā lākou a pau, a luana ihola nō kā lākou huaka'i māka'ika'i.

A ma hope o ka luana nui 'ana, 'ōlelo maila 'o Ka'ehuikimanōopu'uloa i mua o ke ali'i a akua ho'i, "I kipa mai nei au i ou lā no ke kauoha a kahi kauā lepo āu, i ku'u lā i hānai 'ia ai e ia."

'Ae maila ke ali'i me ka 'olu'olu, a nīnau mai, "Pehea lā wau e hana aku ai iā 'oe, e ku'u mo'opuna?"

'Ōlelo akula ua wahi hū'eu nei, "E hā'awi mai i mana a me ona ikaika, i koa a i mau kino lehulehu no'u, a e kau mai nā halo ou ma luna o ku'u po'o me ka poni 'ana ia'u mai luna a lalo."

Ka'ehuikimanōopu'uloa and his fellow sharks slept until daybreak, and their morning meal was already prepared. After it was finished, they immediately set off for Kaho'olawe, where Kamohoali'i, the shark god of the ocean, dwelled. They met with the outer guard, asking, "Is the old man in residence?"

"Yes," the guard replied.

"Then go and tell my godly guardian that I, Ka'ehuikimanōopu'uloa, child of Kapukapu and Hōlei, am here. I am the guard of Pānau cliffs in Puna and am here with the chiefs of Hawai'i, humble servants who have come to visit him. Tell him the nature of the journey that has brought us before his royal court."

The guard then went to Kamohoali'i and told him all that was said. The chief answered, "Bring them and welcome them." Ka'alamikihau, the shark chief of Honua'ula, fetched Ka'ehuikimanōopu'uloa and his party and led them into a grand cavern adjacent to the one where Kamohoali'i resided. As they entered, a feast was prepared through Ka'alamikihau's ministrations. They all took part and afterwards enjoyed the rest of the evening in comfort. Then the chief's messenger announced, "The old man is coming to see you." At that very moment, Kamohoali'i entered, his back overgrown with seaweed and barnacles. He greeted each member of the party.

After much socializing, Ka'ehuikimanōopu'uloa spoke directly to the godlike chief, saying, "I have come here to see you on the instructions of a servant of yours, given during the time he raised me."

The chief graciously assented and asked, "How can I accommodate you, my grandchild?"

The little one replied, "Grant me power, strength, bravery, and a multitude of bodies so that I might be fearless, and lay your fins on my head, anointing me from head to toe."

The *mo'olelo* of Ka-'ehu-iki-manō-o-Pu'uloa (the small reddish shark of Pu'uloa) was first written down by William Henry Uaua and published as a serial in the Hawaiian-language newspaper *Ke Au 'Oko'a.* The legend relates the adventures of Ka'ehuikimanōopu'uloa as he travels the length of the Hawaiian chain. Born of human parents, Ka'ehuiki emerged from the womb in the form of a baby shark. When he grew older, he undertook a *ka'apuni,* a chiefly tour of the islands, pausing to pay his respects to the shark *ali'i* of the districts he visited. This excerpt tells of Ka'ehuiki's visit to the shark god Kamohoali'i at his sea cave on the island of Kaho'olawe. Elder brother of the fire goddess Pele, Kamohoali'i is revered as a deity of great power, and many Hawaiian families look upon him as their *'aumakua* (family god and guardian spirit).

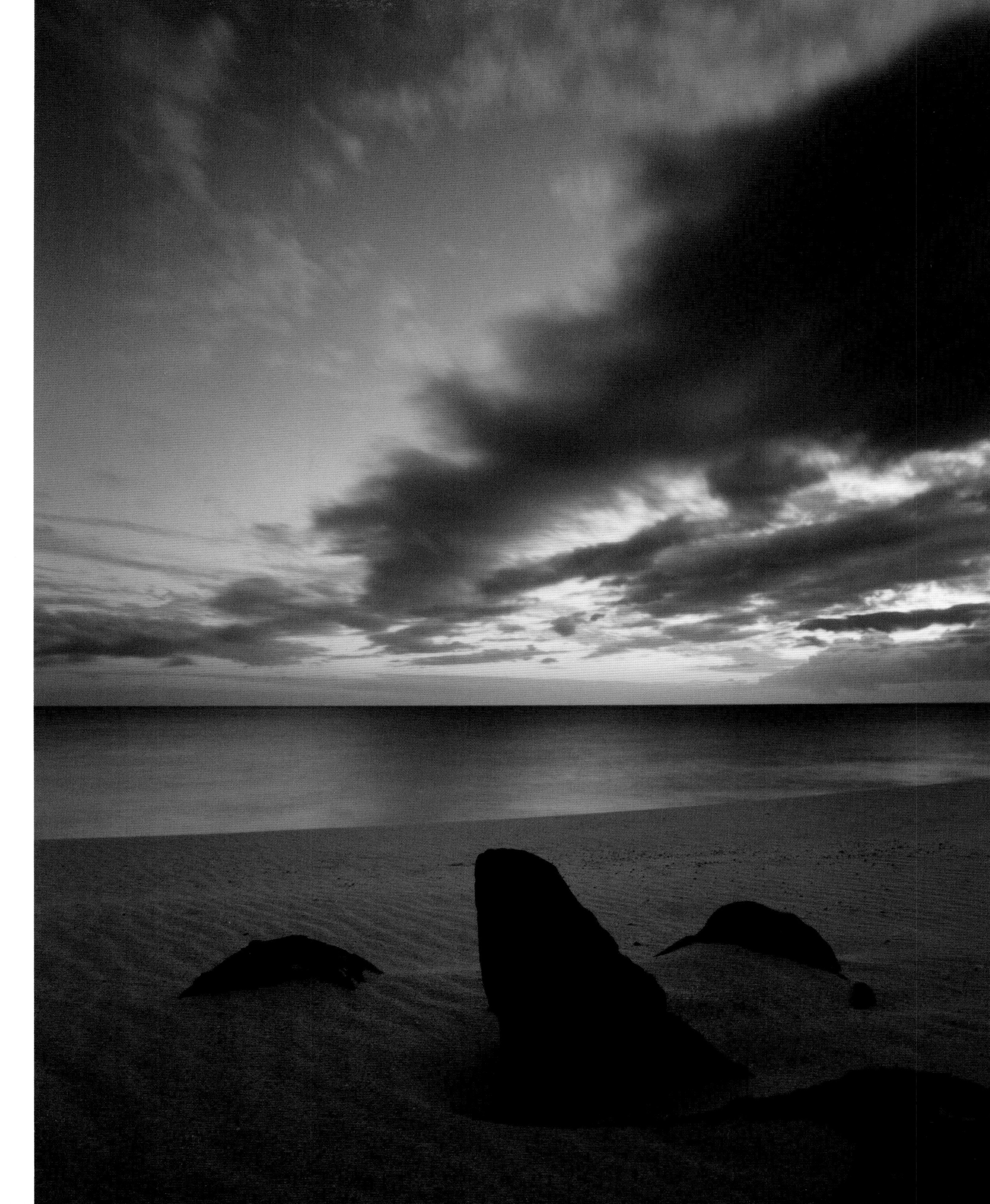

ʻAe maila ka ʻelemakule, "ʻApōpō a kūpono ka lā i ka lolo, ʻo ka manawa ia. I kēlā lā aku, hele ʻoukou."

Pau nā hana o ia pō, moe lākou nei, a ao aʻe, mākaukau nā mea a pau loa no ka pāʻina ʻana. A pau ia hana a lākou, ʻo ka ʻai ʻana, kakali akula lākou nei no ka hana a ke aliʻi ma luna o ua wahi kamaʻeu ʻōpio nei a kākou. A kūpono ka lā i ka lolo, i ia manawa i hiki mai ai ua Kamohoaliʻi nei ma ko lākou nei wahi me ka weliweli ano akua, me nā manō aliʻi a pau ma hope ona me ko lākou mau kāhiko ʻano ʻē ma nā kino mai luna a lalo, a komo maila ʻo Kaʻalamikihau me ka huewai poni i kama ʻia i ka ʻaha a paʻa. I ia manawa, kiʻi akula ʻo Kaʻalamikihau iā Kaʻehuikimanōopuʻuloa, a alakaʻi maila i mua o ke aliʻi. Kū ihola kēlā me ka wiwo ʻole i mua o nā mea a pau loa a me ke akua hoʻi. Kau maila nā halo o Kamohoaliʻi i luna o ua wahi kamaʻeu ʻōpio nei, a ninini maila ʻo Kaʻalamikihau i ka huewai poni ma luna o ke poʻo, a puana aʻela i nā huaʻōlelo ʻeʻehia weliweli ma kāna hoʻomaikaʻi ʻana ma luna o ke poʻo o ua wahi ʻōpio wiwo ʻole nei a kākou.

E ʻōlelo ana penei: "Ke kau aku nei au, ʻo Kamohoaliʻi, i nā hoʻomaikaʻi ʻana ma luna ou me kēia wai poni iā ʻoe, a ke hāʻawi aku nei au iā ʻoe i ka mana, i ka ikaika a me ke koa lua ʻole ma kēia moana pālahalaha, mai ka hikina a ke komohana, mai ka ʻākau a ka hema, ma nā wahi a pau āu e hele ai, ʻaʻole kekahi mea e lanakila ma luna ou, mai kēlā paia lani a kēia paia lani, a hiki i nā kūkulu o Kahiki; ʻo nā kupu, ʻo nā ʻeu o ka moana e ʻaʻa mai iā ʻoe ma ke ʻano hakakā, he mea ʻole lākou a pau i mua ou, he noho mālie ko lākou ola, hoʻopaʻipaʻi mai iā ʻoe, ʻo ko lākou make ia, a ke hāʻawi aku nei au i mau kinolau nou, (hoʻokahi haneri ka nui), aia a manaʻo aʻe ʻoe i kou kino e lilo i kino humuhumu, ua lilo aʻela pēlā, a i kino pokipoki, pēlā aku a haneri ka nui o kou mau hoʻololi ʻana, ʻo ia kou mau kinolau aʻu e hāʻawi nei ma koʻu ʻano akua, a mana hoʻi, a e ola mau loa ʻoe a kau i ka puaneane, ua noa, lele wale."

I kēlā lā e kau nei nā hoʻopomaikaʻi ma luna o ia nei, ua maluhia ke anaina, me ka weliweli lua ʻole, a pau aʻela nā hana o ia manawa, hoʻi aʻela ka ʻelemakule me kona pūʻali aliʻi a pau, a noho ihola lākou nei malihini me ke kamaʻāina hoʻokahi ʻo Kaʻalamikihau, a lilo aʻela ʻo Kaʻehuikimanōopuʻuloa i mea kiʻekiʻe loa i mua o kona poʻe hoa hele me ka makaʻu a me ka weliweli ʻia e lākou nei.

ʻŌlelo maila ʻo Kaʻalamikihau i mua o nā aliʻi malihini, "ʻAkahi nō au a ʻike i ka hana i hana ʻia iho nei i mua o ia ala, ʻaʻole ma mua a hiki i kēia lā wale nō; he nui koʻu weliweli a me ka makaʻu no nā mea i hana ʻia, a me ka hāʻawi ʻana i nā kinolau."

The lord agreed, saying, "Tomorrow when the sun is directly overhead will be the appropriate time. You will all leave the next day."

When everything was done that evening, they slept, and at dawn the next day, their morning meal was ready. After eating, they waited patiently for Kamohoaliʻi to bless our lively hero. When the sun was directly overhead, Kamohoaliʻi arrived in all his terrifying glory, accompanied by shark chiefs adorned from head to toe in strange garments. Kaʻalamikihau entered with the anointing gourd tightly bound in sennit and took Kaʻehuikimanōopuʻuloa to the chief. He stood fearlessly before the god and all the others in attendance. Then, while Kaʻalamikihau poured the contents of the anointing gourd over his head, Kamohoaliʻi put his fins upon the lively little one, uttering solemn and profound words as he laid his blessing upon our fearless little hero.

The following was spoken: "I, Kamohoaliʻi, bestow blessings upon you and with this water anoint you. I grant you power and strength with courage unmatched throughout this broad ocean—from east to west, from north to south, to all the places you will travel. There is no one who will triumph over you, from one horizon to the other, to the borders of Kahiki. Any upstarts or mischief-makers of the ocean who dare to fight with you—they will be nothing in your presence. Silence is their life, contention their death. Further, I grant you a multitude of body forms. When you desire to take the form of a humuhumu, *your body will become so, likewise a crustacean's body, and so on. One hundred is the number of your transformations. These body forms I am granting you with my godlike powers. May you live to a ripe old age. The* kapu *is removed, it is flown."*

As the blessing was bestowed, the crowd was calm, filled with respectful reverence. When the deed was done, the old one and his royal army retired while the newcomers remained with the sole resident, Kaʻalamikihau. Kaʻehuikimanōopuʻuloa became truly exalted before his terrified and awe-struck companions.

Kaʻalamikihau spoke before the visiting chiefs: "This is the first time I have seen such an event. I am full of awe at what happened and at the bestowing of the body forms."

The newcomers agreed, replying, "We were fortunate to experience this great event."

At this time Kaʻalamikihau prepared food and urged the newcomers to eat, and when the meal was finished, it was time for them to relax comfortably until nightfall. Before the day ended, however, there was an evening feast, and when it was finished, Kaʻalamikihau said to them, "I would like to join your sightseeing trip. The only problem is our chief's refusal."

Kepanilā answered, "You shouldn't leave our chief because you are the true steward of his royal court. You have become a highly honored person. There are other chiefs below you, and it is through your orders that they all obey. This we see."

Kaʻalamikihau agreed, "Yes, it is my duty to host all newcomer chiefs like you and to prepare everything until they depart from this royal court."

They slept that night, and when it dawned, it was their day to depart. Kaʻalamikihau prepared food for breakfast, and when the meal was finished, he made an announcement from the royal court: "Our ruling chief is entering to see you all, expressing his deep appreciation." Then Kamohoaliʻi came in with his retinue.

He uttered his royal proclamation: "I have come today to meet again with you all, the chiefs of Hawaiʻi, to let you go with my utmost blessing. Your royal trip to visit my court has honored us indeed. There has never before been a royal visit to my place like yours these past days. I now release you with my blessing and that of my court. Travel to the borders of Kahiki, and when you return, you must visit together with us here."

Kaʻehuikimanōopuʻuloa responded to the chief's speech. "Oh, King of Kings, God of the great, wide ocean from the horizon to the shores of Kahiki, I humbly offer our thanks for your royal speech today. We are traveling on like the sun setting in the west, and we place our trust in you during this journey to the sacred bounds of Nuʻumealani. When we return, we will surely remember your royal command about visiting your court."

At that point, everyone bid farewell to the high chief and his court, and the newcomers emerged from the cave, attended by the grand steward, Kaʻalamikihau, who saw them off.

ʻAe like maila nā malihini a pau me ka ʻī mai, "ʻO kākou like ka i komohia i loko o kēia hana nui i hana ʻia iho nei."

I ia wā, ʻo ka hoʻomākaukau maila nō ia o Kaʻalamikihau i nā mea ʻai a hoʻolale akula i nā aliʻi malihini e ʻai lākou, a pau ka ʻai ʻana he manawa luana iho ia no lākou nei a hiki i ka pō ʻana; ma mua naʻe o ko lākou moe ʻana, ʻo ka pāʻina ahiahi ka hana mua, a pau ka ʻai ʻana, ala akula lākou nei a hiki i ka wā moe, pane maila ʻo Kaʻalamikihau iā lākou nei, "ʻO wau kekahi i makemake i kā ʻoukou huakaʻi mākaʻikaʻi, ʻo ka ʻae ʻole mai o ka haku o kākou ka hewa.

I ia wā i ʻōlelo mai ai ʻo Kepanilā, "ʻAʻole ʻoe e pono ke haʻalele i ko kākou haku aliʻi, no ka mea, ʻo ʻoe maoli nō ka puʻukū o kona alo aliʻi, a ua lilo ʻoe i mea hanohano nui loa, a he mau aliʻi ʻē aʻe ma lalo mai ou; ma kāu mau ʻōlelo lākou a pau e hoʻolohe mai ai a mākou e ʻike aku nei."

ʻAe maila ʻo Kaʻalamikihau, "ʻAe, ʻo kaʻu mau hana ihola kēia ʻo ka hoʻokipa mai i nā malihini aliʻi a pau, a me ka hoʻomākaukau ʻana i nā mea ʻai a pau a hiki i ka wā e kaʻawale aku ai lākou a pau mai kēia alo aliʻi aku e like me ʻoukou."

Moe lākou nei i ia pō, a ao aʻe, ʻo ko lākou nei lā ia e hele ai; ua mākaukau mua ka puʻukū Kaʻalamikihau i nā mea ʻai o ka ʻaina kakahiaka, ʻo ka ʻai nō ia a pau ka ʻai ʻana, haʻi maila ʻo Kaʻalamikihau i ka ʻōlelo mai ke alo aliʻi mai. "E komo mai ana ke aliʻi haku o kākou, e ʻike iā ʻoukou me ka mahalo nui." I ia wā komo mai ana ua Kamohoaliʻi nei me kona mau pūʻali aliʻi a pau.

A pane maila i kāna ʻōlelo aliʻi; "Ua hiki mai nei au e hālāwai hou me ʻoukou, nā aliʻi o Hawaiʻi, i kēia lā, no ka hoʻokuʻu ʻana aku me kuʻu mahalo nui. Ua hoʻohanohano mai kā ʻoukou huakaʻi aliʻi ma ke kipa ʻana mai i koʻu alo aliʻi nei; ʻaʻole he huakaʻi aliʻi nui i kipa mai ma mua i koʻu wahi nei e like me ʻoukou i kēia mau lā, a ke hoʻokuʻu aku nei au iā ʻoukou me kuʻu mahalo nui, a me koʻu pūʻali aliʻi. E hele ʻoukou a hiki i nā kūkulu o Kahiki a i hoʻi nui mai e kipa nui mai ma ʻaneʻi."

Pane maila ʻo Kaʻehuikimanōopuʻuloa no ka haʻiʻōlelo a ke aliʻi. "E ka Moʻī o nā Moʻī, ke Akua hoʻi o kēia moana nui laulā, mai nā paia lani a kūkulu o Kahiki, ke waiho haʻahaʻa aku nei au i ko mākou mahalo nui i ka lohe ʻana i kāu ʻōlelo aliʻi o kēia lā; ke hele aku nei mākou ma mua e like me ka lā e iho ana i ke komohana, a e hilinaʻi nui mākou ma luna ou ma kēia hele ʻana a hiki i ka peʻa kapu o Nuʻumealani, a huli hoʻi mai mākou e hoʻomanaʻo mau nō mākou i kāu kauoha aliʻi ma ke kipa ʻana mai ma kou alo aliʻi nei."

I ia manawa aloha like akula lākou nei a pau i ke aliʻi nui me kona pūʻali aliʻi, a puka nui maila nā malihini me ka ukali ʻana mai a ka puʻukū nui Kaʻalamikihau, a hoʻokuʻu maila ʻiā lākou nei e hele.

Ka Lawaiʻa ʻOpihi

ʻO kahi lawaiʻa kēia, pau kāne me ka wahine, me kamaliʻi, me ke aʻo mua ʻole; ke hiki nō i kahi o ka ʻopihi, he pōhaku nō, he lāʻau, aia ka pono ʻo ka loaʻa; ʻaʻole hoʻi pēlā ka poʻe i ʻike i ke kuʻi ʻopihi. ʻO ka ʻopihi makaiauli, ʻo ia ka ʻopihi loaʻa i kamaliʻi, ma ka pali o Kaholo, Lānaʻi, kahi kaulana i kēia mea he ʻopihi; he ʻoiaʻiʻo nō ia, akā ma ka nunui o ka ʻopihi, ʻaʻole e loaʻa aku ʻo Kanapou, Kahoʻolawe. Ma Kahoʻolawe ua kamaʻāina kēia mau wahi i ko ʻoukou mea kākau, akā, ma ka nunui, ʻaʻole e loaʻa aku kēlā wahi ʻo Kanapou, ʻo ia kēlā kahawai nui e huli pono lā i Honuaʻula. Ua like ka ʻopihi me ke bola o kauhale kūʻai, ʻaʻole hoʻi ʻo ke bola nunui, ʻo ka mea kuʻu iki a ua hiki nō ka ʻiʻo kao ke kupa ʻia a moʻa i loko o ka ʻopihi, ʻo ka ʻiʻo pipi hapahā o mākou o Lahaina nei, ua lawa ia ke kupa ʻia a pau i loko o ka ʻopihi o kēlā wahi; ʻaʻole nō he ʻopihi luʻu, akā, he ʻopihi nō e kau ana i kahakai pali. He hoʻokahi pule ka noho ʻana o ko ʻoukou mea kākau i laila, me ka ʻai ʻole i ka ʻai; ʻo ka wai, ʻo ka iʻa, ʻopihi, kao, ʻo ia wale nō ka ʻai. A pēlā i ʻike ʻia, ʻo ia kahi o ka ʻopihi nunui a he nui nō ke dālā loaʻa mai no ka ʻopihi, a ua ʻike ko Honolulu poʻe i ka waiwai o ia lawaiʻa, he mau kāuna ʻopihi nō i kahi pā liʻiliʻi, he hapahā nō ke kumu kūʻai, a i makemake ʻoukou e ʻike i kēlā ʻopihi nunui, e holo nō i laila i pau kuhihewa. A malia paha he kānalua kekahi poʻe heluhelu no ka ʻoiaʻiʻo o kēia, a laila, he mea pono e haʻi aku au i kekahi wahi moʻolelo kahiko o kekahi kanaka, a ʻo ia

---

Hawaiian fisherman A. D. Kahāʻulelio heard the legend of Puʻuiʻaiki from his grandparents and incorporated it in a series of articles on fishing lore that he wrote in 1902 for the Hawaiian-language newspaper *Ka Nūpepa Kūʻokoʻa.* Kahāʻulelio's grandparents had grown up in Honuaʻula, Maui, just across the channel from Kahoʻolawe, and in 1825 moved to the Lahaina area, where "they traded and peddled fish for price; they gave fish in exchange for taro or *paʻiʻai* [undiluted *poi*] from the people of Lahaina." Kahāʻulelio's father was also a fisherman, and he passed on to his son an intimate knowledge of the fishing grounds off Maui, Lānaʻi, and Kahoʻolawe. As Kahāʻulelio noted in *Ka Nūpepa Kūʻokoʻa,* "The sea all around Kahoʻolawe has been fished in by your writer with his parents and grandparents." Kahāʻulelio recalled the tale of Puʻuiʻaiki in order to explain the large size of *ʻopihi makaiauli* (bluish-gray fleshed limpets) found on the rocks at Kanapou bay.

While some elements of his tale are strongly reminiscent of "Kaʻao no Kalaepuni," others appear to have been borrowed from the well-known legend "Moʻolelo no Punia," published in the *Fornander Collection of Hawaiian Antiquities and Folk-lore.* Kahāʻulelio's description of the spring at Kanapou conforms with other accounts of traditional Hawaiian waterholes, which were shallow pits rather than deep-shafted wells. Hawaiian scholar Mary Kawena Pukui translated Kahāʻulelio's entire series of articles, and this story has been lightly adapted from her work.

ʻOPIHI FISHING

This is a kind of fishing that all men, women, and children can do without being taught. When you get to where the ʻopihi *are you can use a rock, a stick, whatever is handy, but that is not how the people who know how to pound* ʻopihi *do it. The dark* ʻopihi makaiauli *were gathered by children at the cliffs of Kaholo, Lānaʻi, a place famed for its* ʻopihi. *True, but for size they were not equal to those of Kanapou, Kahoʻolawe. Your writer is well acquainted with these places. For bigness, they do not compare to Kanapou's. It is at that large stream facing Honuaʻula [Maui]. The* ʻopihi *are as large as the bowls found in shops, not large ones, but the smaller ones. Goat meat could be boiled in* ʻopihi *shells and twenty-five cents worth of beef bought in Lahaina could be cooked entirely in* ʻopihi *shells from that locality—not the* ʻopihi *dived for but those which clung to the sea cliffs. Your writer was there for a week without vegetable food, living only on water, fish,* ʻopihi, *and goat meat. That is how I discovered that that was the place of large* ʻopihi. *Much money is gained by selling* ʻopihi, *and Honolulu's people know the value of this food, for they get only a few times four* (mau kāuna) ʻopihi *in a saucer for the price of twenty-five cents. If you wish to see those large* ʻopihi, *go there and see for yourself. Perhaps some will doubt the truth of this statement, so it will be well for me to tell an old story of a certain man. He caused the largeness of the* ʻopihi *of this place, so my grandparents told me.*

A certain man of Hawaiʻi named Puʻuiʻaiki left Kohala on his small canoe, and halfway across the ʻAlenuihāhā channel, his canoe was swamped by the waves, and he could not make it move. He tried to float it and, failing, decided it would be better to swim to Kahoʻolawe. The wind blew him along and the swimming was easy. As he swam, an ʻopihi makaiauli *appeared before him. He said to himself,*

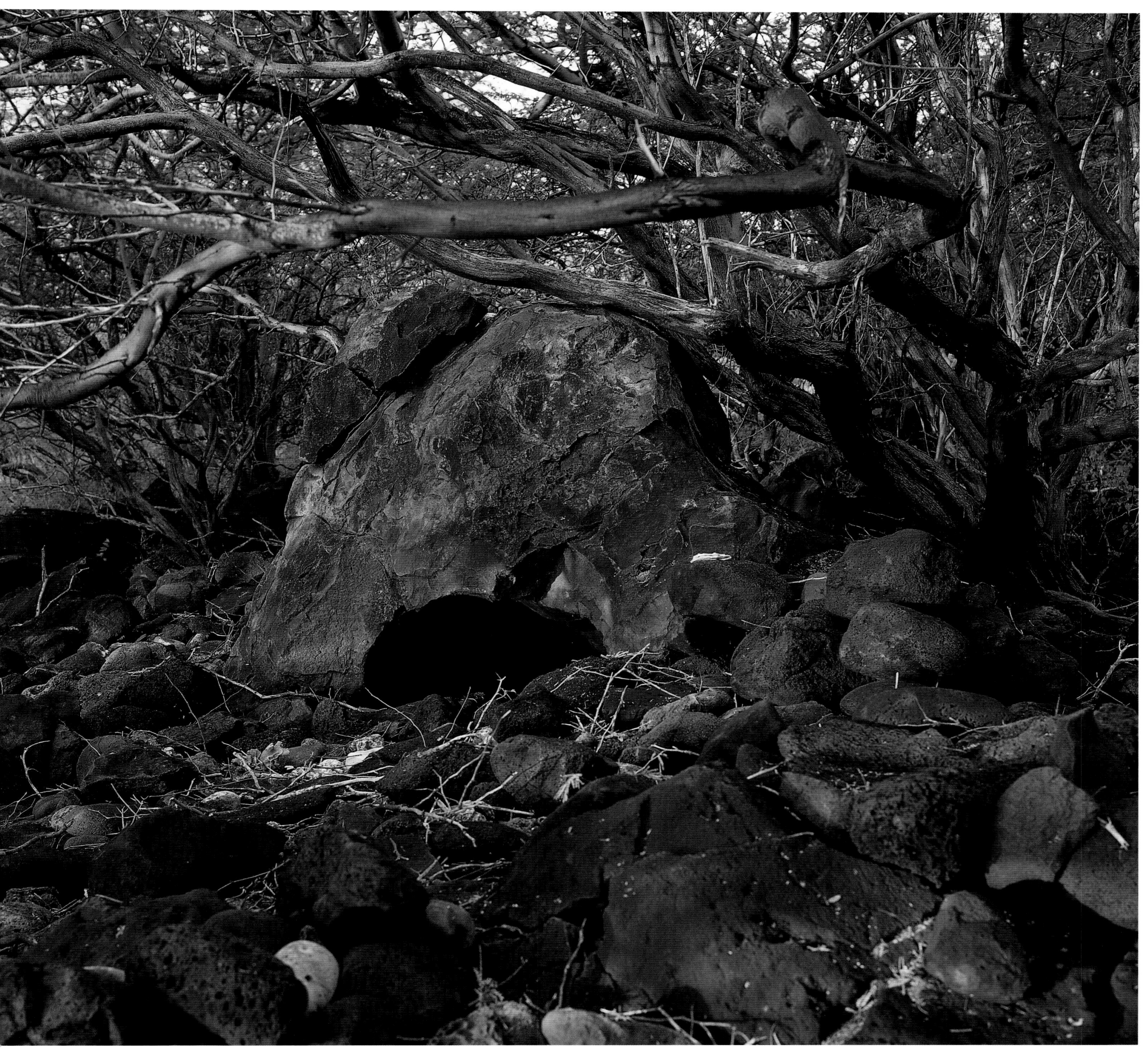

Preceding pages ⟲

A scatter of fire-cracked stones and sun-bleached shells reveals the location of an ancient campsite on Kahoʻolawe's upper slopes. Though the island's early inhabitants got the bulk of their food from the sea, most families probably spent at least a few months of each year cultivating dryland crops in fields on the flanks of Moaʻulanui. Remnants of their temporary camps can be found throughout the island's eastern interior.

kā ke kumu i nunui ai ka ʻopihi o ia wahi, a koʻu mau kūpuna i haʻi mai iaʻu.

He wahi kanaka no Hawaiʻi, ʻo Puʻuiʻaiki ka inoa, ua haʻalele ʻo ia iā Kohala ma luna o kona wahi waʻa; a ma waenakonu o ʻAlenuihāhā, ua poʻipū ʻia ihola kahi waʻa e nā ʻale, a make kahi waʻa. Ua noke kēia i ka hoʻolana, a hiki ʻole, hoʻoholo ihola kēia e ʻau mai i Kahoʻolawe ka pono; ʻo ka puhi mai o ka makani, he maʻalahi ka ʻau ʻana mai. Iā ia nei nō e ʻau mai ana, lana ana kēia wahi ʻopihi makaiauli ma mua pono o ia nei, ʻī ihola kēia i loko iho ona, "He keu hoʻi kēia o kahi ʻopihi kūpaianaha, ʻaʻole kā hoʻi he pono iho i loko o ke kai, pehea lā ke ʻano a me ka manaʻo o kēia wahi ʻopihi?" Ko Puʻuiʻaiki lālau akula nō ia a paʻa i ko ia nei lima, me ka nīnau mau ʻana i ke ʻano a me ka hana a kēia wahi ʻopihi makaiauli. E ka poʻe heluhelu, he ʻoiaʻiʻo, he wahi ʻopihi kēia i hoʻouna ʻia mai e ka makāula Moaʻula, a ʻo ia nō kēlā wahi puʻu e kū lā i luna o Kahoʻolawe, a ʻo ko laila wahi mauna ihola nō ia; no kona aloha iā Puʻuiʻaiki, hoʻouna ʻo ia i kēia wahi ʻopihi i hoʻopakele nona. E haʻalele kākou i ka moʻolelo o kahi ʻopihi, a e nānā aʻe kākou iā Puʻuiʻaiki e ʻau nei.

Ma hope koke iho nō o ka lālau ʻana o ua wahi Puʻuiʻaiki nei i ka ʻopihi, kāʻalo ana kēia manō nui, a e hāmama pono mai ana ka waha, ʻo ke ā i luna i ka ʻili kai, ʻo ke ā lalo i ka hohonu o ka moana. I ia wā, pane akula ʻo Puʻuiʻaiki: "Inā e nahu ana ʻoe iaʻu, ola au; a inā e moni ana ʻoe iaʻu a komo i loko o ka ʻōpū, a laila make au;" ʻo ke poholo akula nō ia i loko a komo akula ʻo Puʻuiʻaiki i loko o ka ʻōpū o ua manō nei me kēia wahi ʻopihi. Hoʻomaka kēia e waʻuwaʻu i ka ʻiʻo o ua manō nei; ʻekolu nō hoʻi pō,ʻekolu ao, pae ana ua manō nei i ke awa o Kanapou ma Kahoʻolawe, make nō hoʻi ua manō nei. ʻŌʻili akula nō hoʻi ʻo Puʻuiʻaiki, ua hele nō hoʻi ke poʻo a ʻōhule, hinuhinu, a hoʻomaka akula kēia e piʻi mai kahakai aku a ka ʻākulikuli e hihi ana i ke one; hoʻomaha ihola kēia i ka lau pōhuehue a kau ma luna o ke poʻo, ʻike mai nei kānaka lawaiʻa i ko ia nei noho, hoholo mai nei e ʻike iā ia nei me ke ʻano makaʻu, me ka manaʻo he pupule. "Aloha ʻeā," wahi a kānaka lawaiʻa.

"ʻAe, aloha nō, ʻeā! He wahi wai no ko ʻoukou?"

"ʻAʻole o mākou wai, akā, aia nō ka pūnāwai ma uka aʻe nei, inā ʻoe e makemake, a laila, alakaʻi aku mākou iā ʻoe."

"ʻAe," wahi a ua Puʻuiʻaiki nei, "E hoʻomaha aʻe hoʻi a ʻoluʻolu, a laila, piʻi aku au."

I kānaka lawaiʻa i hoʻi aku ai, pane aʻe nei kahi kanaka, ʻeā, "ʻO kā kākou hana pono wale nō e pepehi kākou iā iā; inā ʻaʻole make kēlā kanaka, e papau

"What a strange ʻopihi *this is. It does not sink into the sea. What kind of thing is this and what does it mean?" Puʻuiʻaiki reached out and grasped it in his hand, as he asked repeatedly what it was about and what this* ʻopihi makaiauli *meant. O readers, in truth this was an ʻopihi sent by the prophet Moaʻula, and that is the little hill standing on Kahoʻolawe, the only mountain of that land. He was sorry for Puʻuiʻaiki and sent the* ʻopihi *to rescue him. Let us leave the* ʻopihi *and turn to look at Puʻuiʻaiki swimming in the sea.*

Soon after Puʻuiʻaiki had grasped the ʻopihi, *a huge shark came by with his mouth open wide. The upper jaw stretched up to the surface, and the lower jaw reached down into the depths of the sea. Then Puʻuiʻaiki spoke, "If you bite me, I'll live. If you swallow me whole into your stomach, I'll die." Puʻuiʻaiki slipped into the mouth of the shark and down into its stomach still holding onto his* ʻopihi. *There he scraped the flesh of the shark for three nights and three days. The shark beached itself at the bay of Kanapou on Kahoʻolawe and died. Out came Puʻuiʻaiki with a bald, shiny head and went up from the beach to where* ʻākulikuli *weeds crept over the sand. There he rested with* pōhuehue *leaves shading his head.*

Some fishermen saw him sitting there and decided to come take a look at him, yet they were fearful, thinking that perhaps he was crazy. "Aloha," the fishermen greeted him.

"Aloha," he replied, "have you a little water?"

"We have no water but there is a spring above here, if you wish we will lead you there."

"Yes," said Puʻuiʻaiki, "I will rest until I feel better and I'll go up."

As the fishermen went back, one said, "Say, what we should do is kill him. If we do not destroy him, then we ourselves will be destroyed because he is a kupua *[demigod]. His name is Puʻuiʻaiki, but how are we to kill him?"*

"When he goes down to the spring, then we pelt him with stones until they are piled up high beside the spring. Let us go fetch Pu'ui'aiki and ask him how he got here." Pu'ui'aiki told them the story I have mentioned above. They were certain he was a kupua *because the shark had not succeeded in destroying him.*

When they arrived at the spring, which your writer thinks is about four feet deep and nicely dug out, Pu'ui'aiki went down to drink. As he drank, he leaned down with his legs slanted upward. The men began to stone him, but he kept on drinking until stones filled the spring and were heaped high above it.

Strangely, the next morning, when the people went there, the spring was open and the stones were piled on the side toward the upland, for in the meantime the prophet Moa'ula came to get him to go live with him. The spring is open to this day. We got there as castaways in the year 1848 and drank the water of Pu'ui'aiki's spring. If it were not for this spring, we eight would have been corpses, six adults and two of us young boys, one thirteen and your writer, who was then eleven.

This is why the 'opihi *of this place are so large. To make the idea of the size clear: they were as large as the* poi *bowls of Lahainaluna in the olden days and also at this time. Your writer visited Kanapou twice. At other places on Kaho'olawe, the* 'opihi *were the same as everywhere else in the island group. If you wish to see the largeness of the* 'opihi *of that place, let J. K. Nahale buy a steam launch and come to get me. I'll take you to see the famous* 'opihi *of Pu'ui'aiki.*

ana kākou i ka make. He kupua kēlā, 'o Pu'ui'aiki kona inoa, a pehea auane'i kākou e pepehi ai?"

"Aia 'o ia a iho i lalo o ka pūnāwai, a laila, hailuku kākou i ka pōhaku a nui a kū ka paila ma ha'i o ka pūnāwai." Ki'i aku nei lākou iā Pu'ui'aiki, me ka nīnau 'ana, "Pehea 'oe i hiki mai nei i 'ane'i?" A laila, ho'omaka 'o Pu'ui'aiki e hō'ike i ka mo'olelo a kākou e 'ike a'ela ma luna, no laila, maopopo loa ihola iā lākou nei, he kupua 'i'o kēia kanaka, ke make 'ole lā i ka manō.

No laila, i ka hiki 'ana i kahi pūnāwai, me he lā nō, ma ka ho'omaopopo 'ana a kō 'oukou mea kākau, he 'ehā nō kapua'i ka hohonu, ua 'eli ho'ohia 'ia nō. Iā Pu'ui'aiki e iho nei i lalo e inu, kūlou akula nō ho'i kēia e inu, me ka moe lō'ihi nō ho'i o nā wāwae i luna, a 'oiai kēlā e inu ana, ua ho'omaka ihola lākou nei i ka hailuku i nā pōhaku; ke noke lā nō kēlā i ka inu i ka wai, a hiki i ka piha 'ana o ua wahi pūnāwai nei i ka pōhaku, a paila maoli i luna.

Eia na'e ka mea kupanaha, i kekahi kakahiaka a'e, i hele aku ka hana o ua po'e lawai'a nei, e hāmama mai ana ua pūnāwai nei a e kū ana ke āhua o ka pōhaku ma ka 'ao'ao ma uka; eia kā auane'i, ua ki'i maila ka makāula Moa'ula a ua ho'i pū nō lāua i laila e noho ai. Oia mau hāmama nō ko ua pūnāwai lā, a hiki i ko mākou pae 'ōlulo 'ana aku i ka M.H. 1848, a inu nō ho'i i ka wai o ua pūnāwai lā o Pu'ui'aiki, a inā 'a'ole kēlā pūnāwai, a laila he po'e kino kupapa'u mākou a pau 'ewalu, 'eono kanaka makua, 'elua māua mau keiki 'ōpiopio no 'umikūmākolu makahiki o kahi o māua, a no 'umikūmākahi makahiki ho'i o ko 'oukou mea kākau.

A 'o ia ihola ke kumu i nunui ai ka 'opihi o kēlā wahi a 'o ka mea akāka loa, ua like ka nunui o ka 'opihi me ke 'ano bola poi o Lahainaluna i ke au kahiko, a i kēia manawa nō. A no 'elua manawa i kipa ai ko 'oukou mea kākau ma Kanapou; a ma nā wahi 'ē a'e o Kaho'olawe, he like nō ka 'opihi me ko nā wahi 'ē a'e a puni ka pae 'āina, a inā e makemake e 'ike pono i ka nunui o ka 'opihi o ia wahi, e kū'ai nui iho nō e J. K. Nāhale mā i wa'apā mokuahi, a ki'i mai ia'u, na'u ho'i paha ia e lawe aku e hō'ike'ike i ua 'opihi kaulana lā a Pu'ui'aiki.

As Kaho'olawe's upland soils have eroded away, many ancient sites have all but vanished, leaving only scatters of food remains, tools, and other objects lying on the open hardpan. An assortment gathered from one site includes shells of 'awa *(drupe),* pipipi *(periwinkle),* 'opihi *(limpet), and* leho *(cowry), as well as pig teeth, basalt knives, coral files, and a broken* 'ulu maika *(bowling disc).*

E Kanaloa

O KANALOA

Kanaloa o ka wā hala loa

O Kanaloa of the dim past

Hala ka manawa a mākou i kū ai

The time has passed where we existed together.

Kū mākou a kali no ka hōʻailona pono

We rise, waiting for the proper omen

Mai ka makani mai, mai ka moana mai

From the wind, from the ocean,

Maiā Hāloa mai ma ke ala i Kahiki

From Hāloa of the long breath on the trail to Kahiki

No ke ola hou o ka ʻāina, ka ʻāina laʻa o nā akua

For the resurrection of the land, the sacred land of the gods—

O Kāne lāua ʻo Wākea, ke keiki moku a Papa

Of Kāne together with Wākea, the island child of Papa,

Ka ʻāina koʻo o Kāulawahine lāua ʻo Hina

The support of Kāulawahine along with Hina.

ʻO ka naiʻa i ke alo o Maui

The porpoise in the presence of Maui

Ola mau e Kahoʻolawe

Long life, Kahoʻolawe!

Hoʻoikaika ke aloha nou

The love for you is strengthened.

"E Kanaloa" was composed in 1986 by *kumu hula* Pualani Kanahele to be used in ceremonies conducted at the *kuahu* (altar) in Hakioawa pictured at left. The chant calls upon the god Kanaloa, to whom the altar was dedicated, to aid the young activists of the Protect Kahoʻolawe ʻOhana in stopping the U.S. Navy's use of the island as a military training ground and bombing range. The *heʻe* (octopus), laid as an offering atop the altar, is one of Kanaloa's *kinolau.* Kanahele explains that the chant was "designed to go direct to Kanaloa in order to give strength and skill to the defenders of the island."

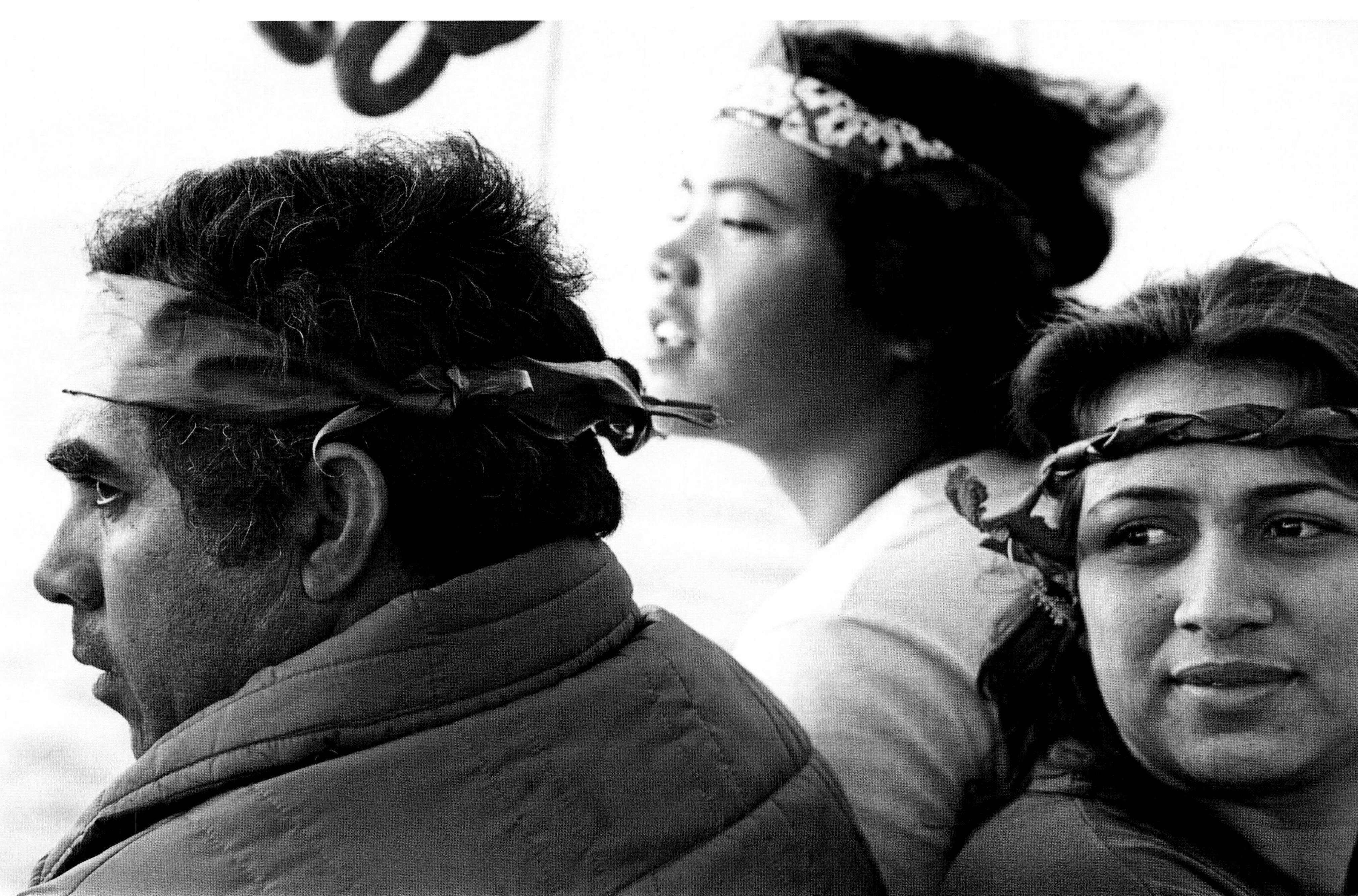

Inā ʻoe e ola hou

Upon your survival

Hoʻomau ke ea o ka lāhui Hawaiʻi i ka ikaika

The life of the indigenous strain will proceed in strength.

E kū me mākou i ke kaua

Stand with us in battle

ʻO ʻoe ke koa, ʻo lākou ka mea heʻe

You are the warrior, they are routed

ʻO ʻoe ka manu, ʻo lākou ka lehua

You are the bird, they are the flower

ʻO ʻoe ka iʻa nui, ʻo lākou ka iʻa liʻi

You are the big fish, they are the small ones.

E Kanaloa, Kanaloa a ka lā maha

O Kanaloa, Kanaloa of the resting sun

Hō mai ka ʻike, hō mai ke akamai

Produce the foresight, produce the accuracy

Hō mai ka ikaika, hō mai ka noʻeau

Produce the strength, produce the skill

I ka heʻe ʻana o ka poʻe ʻē

For casting away the assembly of strangers

Hoʻolohe mai i ka pane

We listen for the reply

E kū me mākou i ke kaua

Stand with us in battle

ʻO ʻoe ke Akua, ʻo mākou ke koa.

You are the God, we are the warriors.

Greg Len Wai, Taiva Wainui, and Carla Ritte, participants in the Protect Kahoʻolawe ʻOhana's first permitted access to Kahoʻolawe, look expectantly toward shore. Since that initial trip in 1976, the ʻOhana has taken over 5,000 people to the island for religious ceremonies, construction and revegetation projects, and educational programs.

Over the years, Kahoʻolawe has suffered enormous environmental damage. Of the many and varied insults the island has endured, the worst were inflicted by introduced grazing animals and military activities.

Following pages ⇾
Fifty years of military usage brought bombing, strafing, shelling by offshore warships, troop maneuvers, even a simulated atomic blast. The effects are visible everywhere on Kahoʻolawe but especially in the central uplands.

This arrow of white-washed stones guided incoming planes to the central "impact zone" that bore the brunt of military assault in recent decades. Though the arrow points straight toward Moaʻulaiki, the peak lies just beyond the target area and escaped significant injury. The adze quarry of Puʻumōiwi unfortunately sits at the heart of the impact zone and did suffer damage.

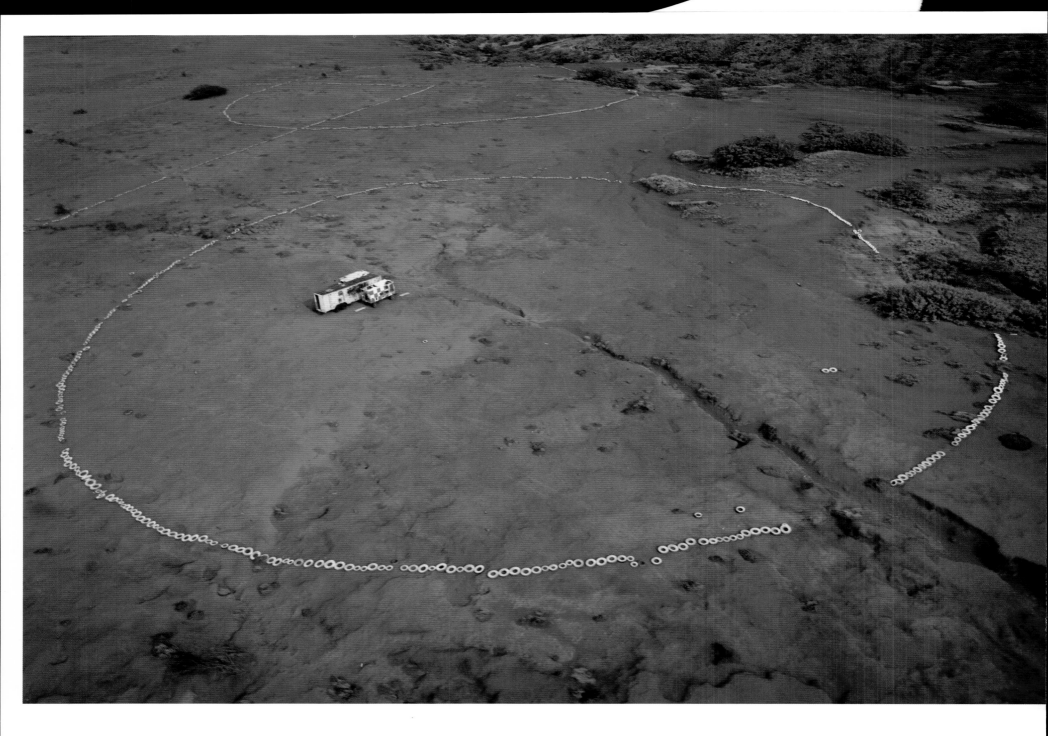

Decommissioned vehicles, such as this battered communications van, were transported to the island and ringed with old tires to serve as bombing targets. The enormous task of removing such debris and clearing the island of unexploded ordnance lies ahead.

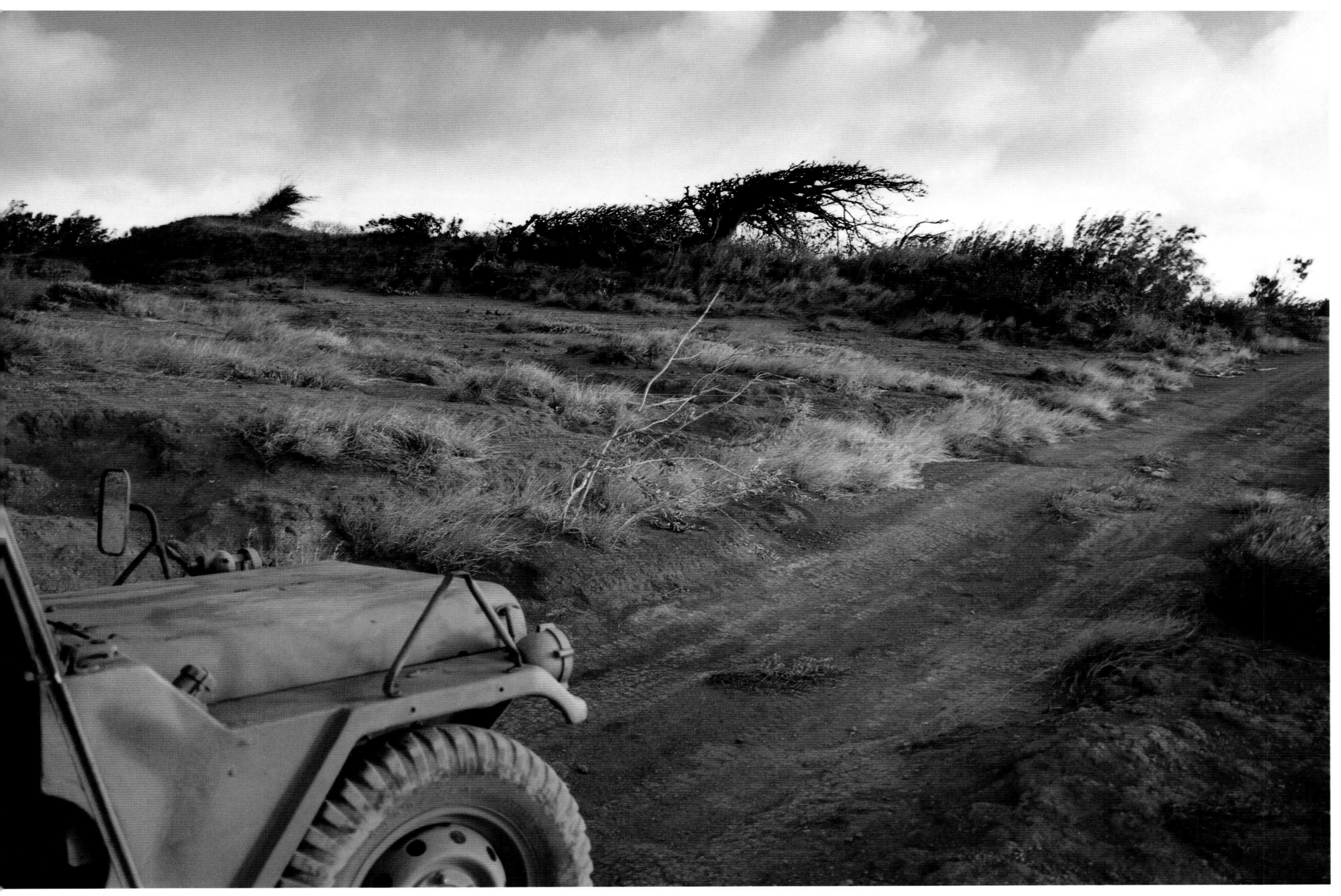

This wind-shaped wiliwili *is one of few survivors from the dryland forest that once grew on Kaho'olawe's upper slopes. Originally, this area was an open, savanna-like landscape with* wiliwili, 'iliahi *(Hawaiian sandalwood), and other hardy trees rising above low shrubs such as* 'akoko *and a thick carpet of* pili. *Though early Hawaiian residents cleared sections of this native forest for cropland, it survived relatively intact until the introduction of goats and other grazing animals in the nineteenth century.*

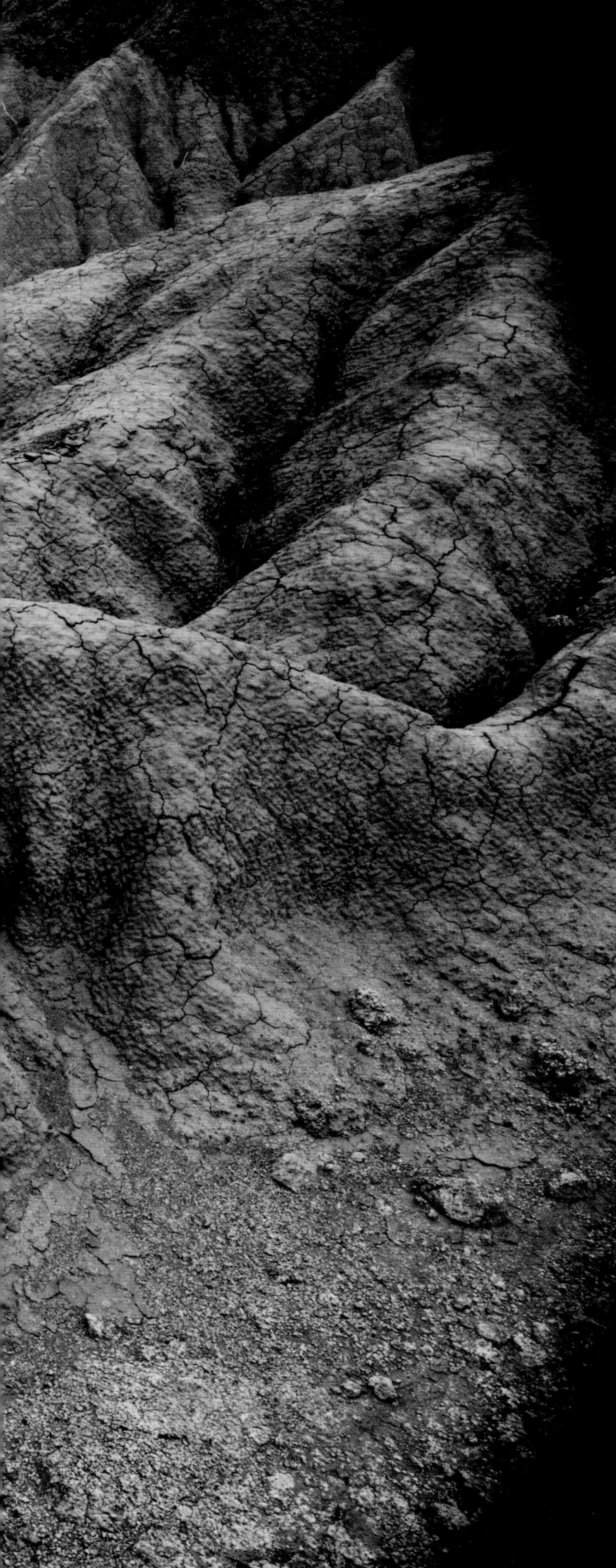

Preceding pages

The loss of its upland vegetation has exposed Kahoʻolawe's soil to the full force of the elements. Winter rains cut deep gullies into the hardpan, washing an estimated 1,900,000 tons of topsoil from the uplands each year and burying valley bottoms beneath thick deposits of alluvium.

Goats, introduced to Kahoʻolawe in the early 1800s, caused the most severe damage to the island's environment. Though the greatest devastation occurred during the ranching period, when up to 40,000 goats roamed the island along with sheep and cattle, overgrazing continued during the military's tenure. Finally, at the ʻOhana's insistence, the goats were eradicated in 1993.

The call of the pū *signals the beginning of Makahiki ceremonies, which honor Lono, god of rain and fertility. Revived in* 1982 *after nearly two centuries, Makahiki—a three-month sequence of ceremonies and celebrations—is now observed on Kaho'olawe every year. As in earlier times, the sounding of the* pū *calls participants to their tasks and signals stages of the ritual.*

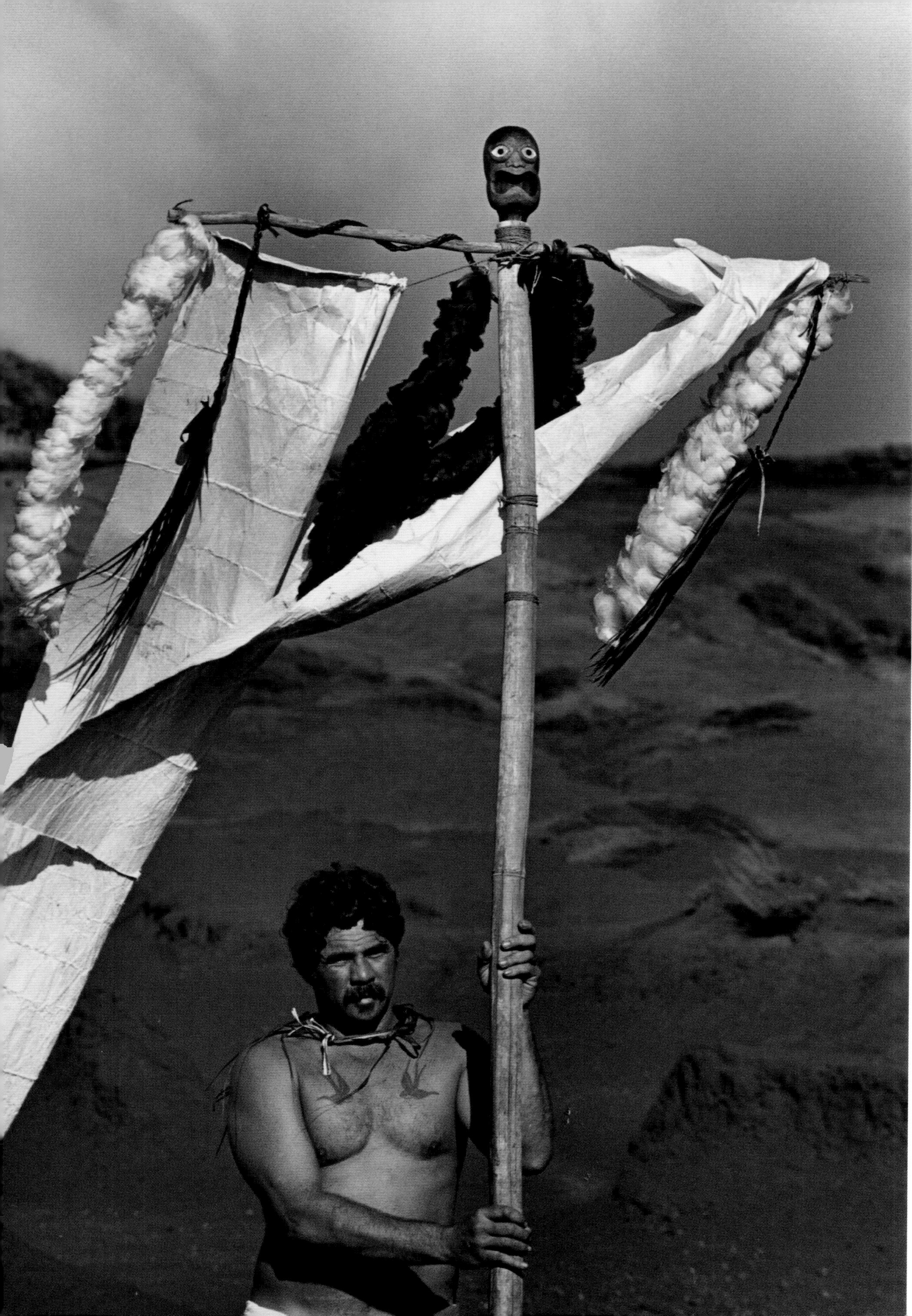

Preceding page

'Ohana members participating in the 1987 Makahiki prepare themselves to carry offerings of niu hiwa *(black coconut),* 'awa *(kava),* kūmū *(goatfish), and* pua'a hiwa *(black pig) wrapped in* kī *leaves to the Hale o Papa (women's temple) and the Hale Mua (men's temple) in the valley of Hakioawa.*

Palikapu Dedman bears the akua loa *(long god), symbol of Lono, at the head of the Makahiki procession. Each year participants cross the island from Hakioawa to Keanakeiki, just as in earlier times* ali'i *(chiefs) and their retinues made a circuit of each of the main Hawaiian islands.*

Kaho'olawe i ka Mālie

KAHOʻOLAWE IN THE CALM

Ma Hakiʻoawa i lohe ʻia ai ka pū

At Hakiʻoawa the conch shell is heard

Aia nā hoʻokupu ma ka Hale o Papa me ka Hale Mua

There are the offerings at Hale o Papa and Hale Mua

Ma Moaʻula i lohe ʻia ai ka pū, aia nā hoʻokupu ma ka lele luna

At Moaʻula the conch shell is heard, there are the offerings at the high altar.

Ma Keanakeiki i lohe ʻia ai ka pū, aia nā hoʻokupu ma ka waʻa

At Keanakeiki the conch shell is heard, there are the offerings in the canoe.

Holo ka waʻa i ke ala i Kahiki

The canoe sails on the path to Tahiti

E hiki hou mai ana ke akua me Makaliʻi, ʻike maka ʻia nā hōʻailona

The god will return again with Makaliʻi, the omens are visible

Ke hoʻoulu nei ʻo Lonoikamakahiki i ka ʻāina

Lonoikamakahiki is greening the land

ʻĀina aloha ʻia e kākou, ʻāina hana ʻino ʻia e nā koa

The land which is loved by all of us, the land which is destroyed by the soldiers

E haʻalele e ka poʻe hana ʻino

Go away, people of destruction!

E mālama, e aloha i ka ʻāina, ʻāina punahele o kākou

Protect and love the land, our beloved land

ʻO Kahoʻolawe i ka mālie.

Peaceful Kahoʻolawe.

Kū Kahakalau, a Hawaiian language instructor from the island of Hawaiʻi, was inspired to compose "Kahoʻolawe i ka Mālie" in 1986 after taking part in ceremonies on Kahoʻolawe marking the close of the Makahiki season. Makahiki, a festival that traditionally begins when the Makaliʻi (the Pleiades) rise at sunset, corresponds to the period of winter rains. It is dedicated to the god Lono, who, in his cloud form, brings life to the crops, and its celebration was reinstituted on Kahoʻolawe beginning in 1982 to secure Lono's help in revegetating the island. Each year the closing ceremonies begin in the valley of Hakioawa, where offerings are left at the Hale o Papa (women's temple) and at the Hale Mua (men's temple). The Makahiki procession, bearing the image of Lono, then proceeds inland to the peak of Moaʻulaiki and down the spine of the island to the beach of Keanakeiki near Laeokealaikahiki. There a *waʻa ʻauhau* (a small, gift-bearing canoe) filled with offerings is set adrift in currents that will, if all goes well, carry it to Lono in Kahiki.

While the Makahiki procession traverses the island on foot, a small fleet of canoes goes a parallel route by sea. The canoes come ashore at the beach of Keanakeiki to rendezvous with the procession for the final ceremony of Makahiki.

A wa'a 'auhau (gift-bearing canoe) waits on the sands of Keanakeiki. Filled with offerings of food, it will be towed out and set adrift on the currents of Kealaikahiki channel to carry its gifts to Lono in distant Kahiki.

He Ko'ihonua no Kanaloa, he Moku

A HISTORY FOR KANALOA, AN ISLAND

'O Wākeakahikoluamea

It was Wākeakahikoluamea

'O Papahānaumoku ka wahine

The wife was Papahānaumoku

Hānau kapu ke kuakoko

The sacred birth pain was born

Ka'ahea Papa iā Kanaloa, he moku

Papa was weak with Kanaloa, an island

I hānau 'ia he punua, he nai'a

It was born a fledging, a porpoise

He keiki i'a na Papa i hānau

A fish child for Papa was born

Holo 'o Haumea i ke keiki moku

Haumea travels to the island child

He moku kapu na Haumea, na Kanaloa

It was a sacred child for Haumea, for Kanaloa

Ho'ono'ono'o kona 'ano wahine

Reflecting her femaleness

Kapa 'ia 'o Kohemālamalama o Kanaloa.

It was known as Kohemālamalama of Kanaloa

Pualani Kanahele composed this chant in 1992 to honor the island of Kaho'olawe and chronicle its history. Like *mele ko'ihonua* proclaiming the ancestry and accomplishments of a ruling *ali'i*, this chant begins by recalling Kaho'olawe's "lineage" and relationship to the gods. Throughout its early verses, Kanahele's *mele* borrows from (and, in so doing, pays tribute to) the chants of earlier composers such as Pāku'i. It also touches upon the various tales and traditions which relate to the island. Among these is the story of 'Ai'ai, son of the fishing god Kū'ulakai and his wife Hinapukui'a. It is said that, after the death of his parents, 'Ai'ai traveled throughout the Hawaiian Islands erecting *ko'a* (fishing shrines) in honor of his parents. One tradition asserts "that he visited Kako'olawe and established a *ko'a kū'ula* at Hakioawa, though it differs from the others, being built on a high bluff overlooking the sea, somewhat like a *heiau* (temple)...wherein the fishermen of that island laid their first fish caught as a thanks offering. *'Awa* and *kapa* were also placed there as an offering to the fish deities." It is possible that the *ko'a* which stands today atop the southern headland of Hakioawa may be the shrine originally erected by 'Ai'ai.

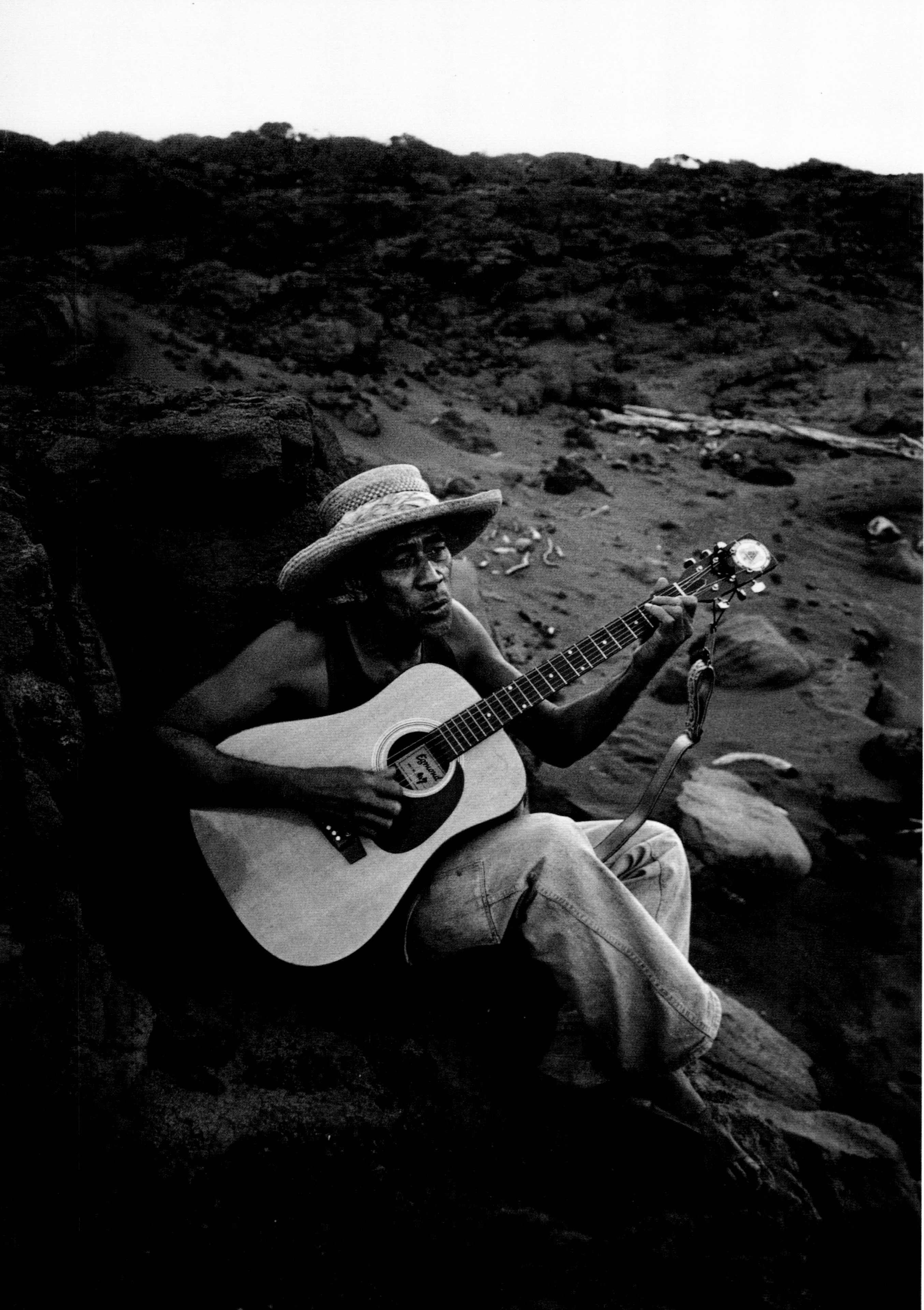

Taro farmer, teach
traditional healer,
Harry Kūnihi Mitc
was mentor to the P
Kahoʻolawe ʻOhana
knowledge guided its
bers in their efforts t
the island, while his
and humor helped th
through profoundly d
times in the early year
their struggle. Here, at H
oawa, he sings his "Mele
Kahoʻolawe," which has
become the unofficial
anthem of the ʻOhana.

E ulu i ka lani a Kāne

To increase towards the heavens of Kāne

E ulu i ke kai a Kanaloa.

To increase in the seas of Kanaloa

Holo mai Pele i ka huakaʻi

Pele travels abroad

Ka huakaʻi ʻimi noho no ka ʻohana

An exploration in search of a family residence

ʻAko ʻia ke ēwe, ʻo Puʻuoinaina

The placenta of Puʻuoinaina was plucked

Na Pele i hoʻolawe i ke keiki

Pele took the child

Ua hoʻolawe ʻia i ke kai ʻo ʻAlalākeiki

It was taken to the sea of ʻAlalākeiki

He hei kapu na Kamohoaliʻi

A sacred place for Kamohoaliʻi

Kapa ʻia ʻo Kahoʻolawe.

Known as Kahoʻolawe

E lana i ka lani a Kāne

To float in the heavens of Kāne

E lana i ke kai a Kanaloa.

To float in the sea of Kanaloa

As the chant continues, it makes reference to significant events of the post-contact period, including the rise of the Kamehameha dynasty, the abandonment of the ancient gods, and the casting down of the *kapu*—the system of traditional social and religious laws that governed Hawaiian society. This third event is referred to as "the time of free eating," for the first *kapu* broken was one forbidding males and females from eating together.

Against this backdrop is set the story of Kahoʻolawe's recent history: the island's use first as a penal colony, then as a ranch (here the name "MacPhee" refers to ranch owner Angus MacPhee), and finally as a military bombing range and training area. In its closing verses, the chant recalls the ceremonies that have been held on Kahoʻolawe over the past decade to revive the life of the island. These include the annual Makahiki festival, reconsecration of the island to Kanaloa, dedication of a *pā hula* (hula platform) named Kaʻieʻie, and the 1992 healing ceremony involving the newly constructed Mua Haʻi Kūpuna ʻo Kahualele (platform of remembrance for the ancestors). "He Koʻihonua no Kanaloa, he Moku" was composed and first performed for this healing ceremony, and was later chanted at the 1994 ceremony transferring control of the island from the United States Navy to the State of Hawaiʻi.

These memorials to George Helm and Kimo Mitchell were laid near Hakioawa in 1987, on the tenth anniversary of their disappearance at sea during an attempt to occupy Kahoʻolawe. Mitchell, Uncle Harry's son, was a young commercial fisherman, planter, and community leader in his native Hāna, while Helm, an outstanding singer and musician from Molokaʻi, was the charismatic president and chief spokesperson of the Protect Kahoʻolawe ʻOhana.

Kaulana ʻo Kanaloa i nā mea lawaiʻa

Kanaloa is famous for fishing techniques

He ʻupena kahe no nā maka iʻa

A flow net for fish

ʻO Kūʻula ka maka iʻa no kēia pae moku

Kūʻula is the revealer of fish for our islands

Ua hahai ke keiki a Kūʻula

The child of Kūʻula reflects his father

Kūkulu aʻe i ke koʻa iʻa

Building fishing memorials [throughout the islands]

A laila nō, koho ʻo ʻAiʻai iā Hakiʻoawa

ʻAiʻai chooses Hakiʻoawa for this shrine

Hoʻomaopopo iā Kūʻulakai, he makua.

In remembrance of the parent, Kūʻula of the sea

He mau maka i ka lani a Kāne

Eyes in the heavens of Kāne

He mau maka i ke kai a Kanaloa.

Eyes in the sea of Kanaloa

ʻO ke au mehameha o Kahoʻolawe

The time of loneliness for Kahoʻolawe

ʻO ke au o nā aliʻi Kamehameha

It is the time of the offspring of Kamehameha

JAMES KIMO MITCHELL
GEORGE JARRETT HELM JR.
MISSING IN THE SEAS OFF KAHO'OLAWE

Ua hōʻea mai nā poʻe haole i kēia ʻāina

Strangers arrived upon this land

A laila, ua lele nā kapu akua

Then the godly laws vanished

ʻO kēia ke au ʻai noa, ʻai hele

This was the time of free eating, eating about

Hōʻea mai i Kahoʻolawe nā mea paʻa ka ʻāina

People arrived on Kahoʻolawe to stay

Kapa ʻia kēia ʻāina, he hale paʻahao.

This land was known as a prison

Ua paʻa i ka lani a Kāne

Kept permanently in the heavens of Kāne

Ua paʻa i ke kai a Kanaloa.

Kept permanently in the sea of Kanaloa

He ʻāina mālama ko MacPhee ʻāilana

A land of caring was MacPhee's island

Mālama i nā poʻe kao, pipi, lio, ʻīlio

To care for the animals, goats, cattle, horses, dogs

Hoʻololi i ke aliʻi kupa i aliʻi haole

The old chiefs lost their status, new chiefs ruled

Ua lawe ʻia mai nā moku kaua

The warships were brought

The surface of a boulder near Laeokealaikahiki tells Kahoʻolawe's history in brief: an ancient petroglyph and a recent bullet hole.

Moku lawe hae, moku lawe koa,

The carriers

Moku lawe pū

The gun boats

Hoʻolawe ʻia ka moku, ʻau i ke kai.

The island eroded, washing out to sea

Hana ʻino i ka lani a Kāne

Mistreated in the heavens of Kāne

Hana ʻino i ke kai a Kanaloa.

Mistreated in the sea of Kanaloa

Ua ala Hawaiʻi mai ka moehewa mai

The Hawaiian woke from the nightmare

Hoʻomaopopo i ke keiki iʻa a Papa

Remembered was the child of Papa

ʻO Kanaloa

O Kanaloa

Ka moku hei a Haumea

The sacred land of Haumea

ʻO Kohemālamalama

O Kohemālamalama

Ke kino o Kamohoaliʻi

The body form of Kamohoaliʻi

E hōʻola kākou iā Kahoʻolawe

Save Kahoʻolawe

High school students pass their bags through unusually gentle surf at Hakioawa. Groups such as these visit the island on monthly, four-day accesses organized by the Protect Kahoʻolawe ʻOhana. Once here, they learn as much as they can about Kahoʻolawe and its traditions and take part in the ʻOhana's ongoing efforts to restore the life of the island.

Ola i ka lani a Kāne

To live in the heavens of Kāne

Ola i ke kai a Kanaloa.

To live in the sea of Kanaloa

Ua kāhea ʻia ʻo Lono i ka makahiki hou

Lono was summoned for a new year

Ma ka Hale Mua o Lono i kāhea ʻia ai

At the Hale Mua of Lono, He was called,

Ua kanaloa ʻo Kanaloa i Kohemālamalama

Kanaloa was reconfirmed to Kohemālamalama

Puka hou aʻe ka mana o Kanaloa

The energy of Kanaloa was revitalized

Ua kani ka leo pahu i ka mālama o Hōkū

The voice of the drum sounded in the care of Hōkū

Kūwāwā i ka houpo a Laka

Resounding in the bosom of Laka

Ua ala ʻo Laka i Kaʻieʻie ma Kanaloa

Laka awoke at Kaʻieʻie at Kanaloa

Ala i ka lani a Kāne

Awaken in the heavens of Kāne

Ala i ke kai a Kanaloa

Awaken in the sea of Kanaloa

Thatched with pili *and* hala *(pandanus) leaves and floored with* ʻiliʻili *(water worn pebbles), this* hale hālāwai *(meeting house) was painstakingly constructed at Hakioawa by ʻOhana members and volunteers. The stalks of* ʻieʻie *and* kī *piled inside were used to decorate the nearby* pā hula *(dance platform), which was completed in 1987 and dedicated to Laka, patron goddess of the* hula.

Following page
In 1992 a Mua Haʻi Kūpuna (platform of remembrance for the ancestors) was constructed on bluffs above Hakioawa. The structure, which faces across the ʻAlalākeiki channel toward Molokini and Haleakalā, was dedicated to those now gone who loved Kahoʻolawe and cared for its lands and waters.

Ua hōʻea ka lā hoʻihoʻi ea

The day for sovereignty is at hand

Ka lā hoʻihoʻi moku

The day to return the island

Ka lā hoʻihoʻi mana kupuna

The day to return the ancestral influence

Aia i ka Mua Haʻi Kūpuna e hānau nei

It is at the Mua Haʻi Kūpuna where it is born

E kanaloa ʻia ana i ka piko o ka pae ʻāina

To be established in the navel of the islands

He ʻāina kūpaʻa no nā Hawaiʻi

A steadfast land for the Hawaiians

E ola ka Mua Haʻi Kūpuna.

Give life to the Mua Haʻi Kūpuna

A mau loa i ka lani a Kāne

Forever in the heavens of Kāne

A mau loa i ke kai a Kanaloa.

Forever in the sea of Kanaloa

Kahoʻolawe Island

N

ʻALALĀKEIKI CHANNEL

KEALAIKAHIKI CHANNEL

Laeokuikui
Waʻaiki
Papakaiki
Papaka
Kaulana
Kūheia
Hakioawa
ʻOawawahie
Luakeālialuna
Puʻukolekole
Puhiokōheohala
Kaukamoku
Ahupū
Ahupūiki
Kiʻi
Laeokaule
MOAʻULAIKI
MOAʻULANUI
1477 FT
Kaluaokamohoaliʻi
ʻOawapālua
Makaʻalae
Luamoaʻula
Pālikalapakea
Honokoa
Kaʻohe
PUʻUMŌIWI
Kanapou
Puhiohālona
Laeohālona
Kaukaukapapa
Luakeālialalo
Keanakeiki
Puʻukamama
Laeokealaikahiki
Kuʻia Shoal
Puʻulaʻi
Kākā
Kamohio
ʻAleʻale
Hanakanaiʻa
Puʻukoaʻe
ʻIliʻililoa
Laeokūakaʻiwa
Laeokākā
Waikahalulu
Wiliwilipeʻapeʻa
Puhianenue

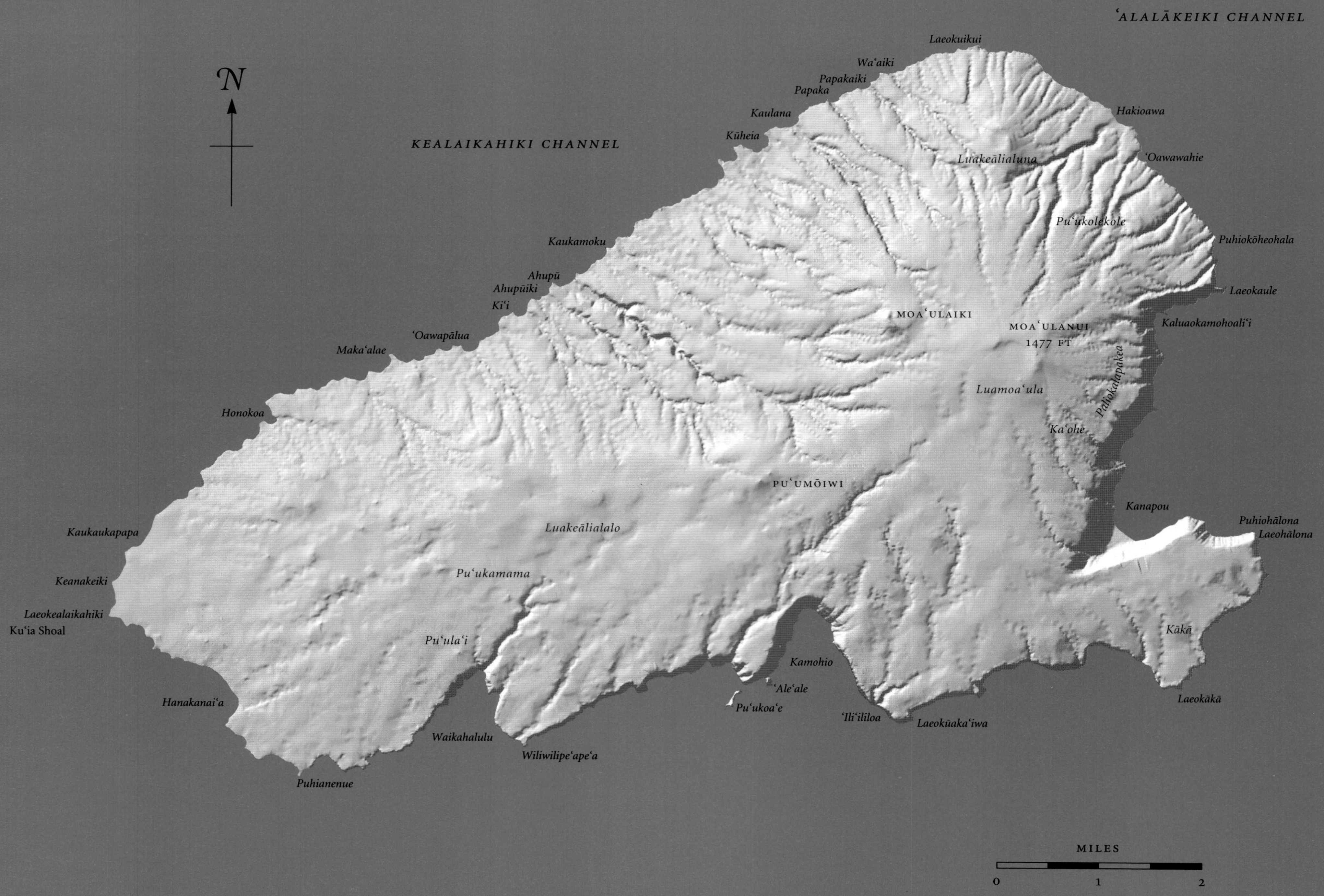

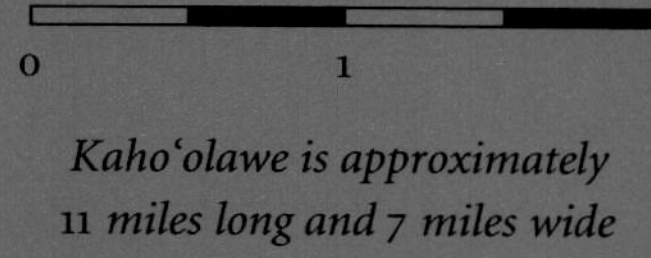

Kahoʻolawe is approximately 11 miles long and 7 miles wide

List of Photographs

Kaho'olawe Chronology

CIRCA A.D. 400
Polynesians settle the Hawaiian archipelago

1027
Earliest existing radiocarbon date for Hawaiian presence on Kaho'olawe

1150–1400
Kaho'olawe figures prominently in voyaging between Hawai'i and the islands of Southern Polynesia

1600
Thriving Hawaiian community on Kaho'olawe by this date

1778
British ships under the command of Captain James Cook enter Hawaiian waters

1779
Following Captain Cook's death, his ships sail past the southwestern tip of Kaho'olawe but sight "neither houses, trees, nor any cultivation"

1793
Maui chief Kamohomoho informs British captain George Vancouver that Kamehameha's wars of conquest have left Lāna'i and Kaho'olawe "nearly over-run with weeds, and exhausted of their inhabitants"

1813
Merchant ship *Lark* runs aground on Kaho'olawe, its surviving crew members probably the first foreigners to set foot on the island

1819
Kamehameha, ruler of the entire Hawaiian chain, dies, leaving his kingdom under the joint control of his son Liholiho and favorite wife, Queen Ka'ahumanu; Liholiho abolishes the traditional system of social and religious laws; *heiau* (temples) are burned and images of the gods overthrown

1820
First Protestant missionaries arrive in Hawai'i

1824
Ka'ahumanu proclaims a missionary-inspired code of laws including threat of "banishment to the island of Tahoorawe [Kaho'olawe]"

1826
First criminals exiled to Kaho'olawe

1828
Lahaina mission station reports Kaho'olawe possesses one school with 28 pupils, adults as well as children

1831
Missionary census estimates a total of 80 inhabitants on Kaho'olawe

1837
Missionary census reports only 20 children on Kaho'olawe, all attending school on the island

1841
Boats from U. S. Exploring Expedition wrecked near western tip of Kaho'olawe; castaways hike to penal settlement of Kaulana, "a collection of eight huts, and an unfinished adobe church" housing 15 male convicts

1848
At the urging of foreign advisors, Kamehameha III institutes the Great Māhele, replacing traditional land stewardship with the western concept of private ownership; Kaho'olawe, among other former crown lands, transferred to the Hawaiian Government

1850
Landing at Hakioawa bay, adventurer Edward Perkins notes large herds of wild goats and their damage to native vegetation

1852
Last prisoner on Kaho'olawe removed due to serious illness

1857
Government inspection finds "some fishermen living on Kahoolawe, maybe not over fifteen, if the men, women, and children are combined"

1858
Government leases Kaho'olawe to R. C. Wyllie, Chancellor of the Kingdom, and Elisha H. Allen, Minister of the Interior, for a period of 20 years, at $505 per year; their surveyor finds 50 Hawaiians in part-time residence

1859
Approximately 2,000 sheep shipped to and released on Kaho'olawe

1864
Elisha H. Allen and C. G. Hopkins obtain new lease for 50 years at $250 per year

1866
Government census records 11 males and 7 females living on Kaho'olawe, 16 of these Hawaiians or part-Hawaiians; all appear to be employed by the sheep ranch

1875
King Kalākaua and his entourage visit the island, noting the presence of "20,000 sheep, 10 horses, 6 native men, 2 white men, 2 full-Hawaiian women, 2 small children, 4 houses, 2 dogs, and a few hundred goat"

1879
Reports of severe overgrazing with "the upper plains entirely denuded of top soil... the whole interior plain has been so swept by wind and floods, that nothing but a very hard red grit is left"

1880
Elisha H. Allen transfers lease title to Albert D. Courtney and William H. Cummins

1884
"Kahoolawe Stock Ranch" listed as possessing "9,000 goats, 2,000 sheep, 200 head cattle, and 40 horses"

1893
With the support of U. S. marines, a Committee of Safety, consisting of white businessmen, overthrows the government of Queen Liliʻuokalani

1898
Hawaiʻi becomes a Territory of the United States

1906
After passing through numerous hands, lease to Kahoʻolawe acquired by Eben P. Low

1910
To prevent further environmental degradation, Gov. Walter F. Frear declares Kahoʻolawe a forest reserve under the control of the Board of Agriculture and Forestry

1913
Scientific expedition from Bernice Pauahi Bishop Museum spends two weeks exploring the island, collecting biological samples and locating a number of ancient Hawaiian sites; John F. G. Stokes, expedition archaeologist, returns to conduct excavations at a fishing shrine in Kamohio bay

1918
Kahoʻolawe withdrawn from forest reserve and leased to rancher Angus MacPhee for 21 years at $600 per year

1920
H. A. Baldwin joins MacPhee to form Kahoolawe Ranch Company

1931
Bishop Museum mounts one-week scientific expedition to Kahoʻolawe; archaeologist Gilbert McAllister subsequently publishes *Archaeology of Kahoʻolawe*, describing 50 early Hawaiian sites

1933
Baldwin and MacPhee obtain second 21-year lease at a rent of $100 per year

1941
U. S. Army signs sublease with Kahoolawe Ranch Company, acquiring bombing rights for $1 per year; *Honolulu Advertiser* reports that Kahoolawe Ranch Co. has reduced resident goat population to 25; after Pearl Harbor attack, martial law declared in Hawaiʻi and Kahoʻolawe appropriated for use as a training ground and bombing target

1942–1945
Kahoʻolawe's southern and eastern cliffs serve as targets for testing of torpedo bombs; beaches of its west end used in dress rehearsals for landings at Tarawa, Okinawa, and Iwo Jima

1953
President Eisenhower signs Executive Order 10436, reserving Kahoʻolawe "for the use of the United States for naval purposes" and placing it under jurisdiction of the Secretary of the Navy; his order also stipulates that the Navy, when it no longer needs the island, will return it in a condition "reasonably safe for human habitation, without cost to the Territory"

1959
Hawaiʻi obtains U.S. statehood

1965
Navy detonates 500 tons of TNT near the bay of Hanakanaiʻa to simulate an atomic blast and observe its effects on ships offshore

1969
Discovery of an unexploded 500-pound bomb in a west Maui field prompts U. S. Representative Patsy Mink to call for the Navy to halt bombing of Kahoʻolawe

1976
Nine native Hawaiians and their supporters make the first of many landings on Kahoʻolawe to protest the Navy's continued use of the island as a bombing target; subsequently the Protect Kahoʻolawe ʻOhana files federal lawsuit charging the U.S. Navy with violating laws pertaining to the environment, historic preservation, and religious freedom

1977
Kimo Mitchell and George Helm lost at sea in the waters off Kahoʻolawe during an effort to protest the bombing; federal court orders the Department of Defense to conduct an inventory of Kahoʻolawe's ancient sites

1980
U. S. Navy and Protect Kahoʻolawe ʻOhana sign a Consent Decree allowing the ʻOhana regular access to Kahoʻolawe for religious, cultural, educational, and restoration activities

1981
Documentation of more than 540 traditional sites results in the entire island being placed on National Register of Historic Places

1982
Protect Kahoʻolawe ʻOhana conducts first traditional Makahiki on Kahoʻolawe since the early 1800s

1990
President Bush issues a memorandum temporarily halting the bombing; U. S. Congress establishes the Kahoʻolawe Island Conveyance Commission "to study and recommend terms and conditions for returning Kahoʻolawe . . . to the State of Hawaiʻi"

1992
Healing ceremony held on Kahoʻolawe to hasten its return to the people of Hawaiʻi

1993
Congress votes to end military use of Kahoʻolawe and authorizes $400 million to clear the island of ordnance; State of Hawaiʻi designates Kahoʻolawe a natural and cultural reserve "to be used solely and exclusively for the preservation and practice of all rights customarily and traditionally exercised by Native Hawaiians for cultural, spiritual, and subsistence purposes"; Kahoʻolawe Island Reserve Commission created to plan for the island's future

1994
Title to Kahoʻolawe officially transferred from the United States military to the State of Hawaiʻi to be held in trust until the formation of "a sovereign Hawaiian nation"

Sources

EPIGRAPH PAGE VII

This chant was first set down in the 1890s by Nathaniel Emerson, an avid collector of traditional *mele.* He included it in an editorial note to David Malo's *Hawaiian Antiquities,* originally published in 1898. See *Hawaiian Antiquities* (Honolulu: Bishop Museum Press, 1991), p. 243, n. 9. Unfortunately, Emerson recorded neither the person from whom he obtained the chant nor any information concerning its origins. The English translation is an adaptation from Emerson.

Ka Mele a Pākuʻi PAGE 5

THE CHANT OF PĀKUʻI

Both the Hawaiian text and the English translation of "Ka Mele a Pākuʻi" are from the *Fornander Collection of Hawaiian Antiquities and Folk-lore.* This nine-volume anthology contains an enormous body of traditional chants, myths, and legends "gathered from original sources" by Judge Abraham Fornander during the 1860s to 1880s. After Fornander's death, his Hawaiian-language manuscripts were acquired by Charles Reed Bishop, who eventually succeeded in getting them rendered into English by a series of translators—Nathaniel B. Emerson, Emma Metcalf Nakuina, and John H. Wise —working under the direction of Dr. W. D. Alexander. The entire collection was published by Bishop Museum Press between 1916 and 1920. "Ka Mele a Pākuʻi" appears in volume IV, part I, pp. 13–16. We have adapted the original translation slightly to conform to modern English usage.

A remarkably similar *mele koʻihonua,* attributed to the poet Kālaikuahulu, also appears in the *Fornander Collection.* Hawaiian scholar Mary Kawena Pukui has suggested that Kālaikuahulu, who served as a priest, genealogist, and counselor to the court of Kamehameha, was the original composer of the chant and that Pākuʻi learned it from him. (See her note in Samuel Kamakau's *Nā Moʻolelo a ka Poʻe Kahiko: Tales and Traditions of the People of Old,* Bishop Museum Press, 1991, pp. 86–87.) It is also possible that the initial verses of the *mele,* which describe the birth of the islands, are of great antiquity and that Kālaikuahulu incorporated them into his chant to increase its *mana* (power). Similar passages appear in a *mele* honoring the birth of Kaumualiʻi, the last paramount chief of Kauaʻi, as well as in chants written for later rulers, including both Kamehameha III and King Kalākaua.

ʻO ka Moʻolelo o Kāne a me Kanaloa PAGE 8

THE TRADITION OF KĀNE AND KANALOA

Kamakau's account of the coming of Kāne and Kanaloa was first published in the January 12, 1867, edition of *Ka Nūpepa Kūʻokoʻa.* It is excerpted from paragraphs 18 and 19 of the tenth section of a much longer article entitled "Ka Moʻolelo o Kamehameha I" ("The Story of Kamehameha I"). The English translation of these paragraphs appears in *Nā Moʻolelo a ka Poʻe Kahiko: Tales and Traditions of the People of Old,* a collection of Kamakau's articles rendered into English by Mary Kawena Pukui (Honolulu: Bishop Museum Press, 1991), p. 112.

Ea mai Hawaiʻinuiākea PAGE 12

THEN AROSE HAWAIʻINUIĀKEA

Like the *mele* of Pākuʻi, Kahakuikamoana's chant was first published in the *Fornander Collection of Hawaiian Antiquities and Folk-lore,* vol. IV, part I, pp. 3–6.

He Mele Pana no Kahoʻolawe PAGE 19

A PLACE-NAME CHANT FOR KAHOʻOLAWE

This chant, and Pualani Kanahele's translation of it, appear in her forthcoming book, *E Mau Ana ʻO Kanaloa, Hoʻi Hou: The Perseverance of Kanaloa, Return!* (Honolulu: ʻAi Pōhaku Press). We are grateful that she has allowed us to publish this and her other chants prior to the book's publication. Pualani has added diacriticals to Kahoʻolawe's place-names where she felt they were appropriate.

He Moʻolelo no Molokini PAGE 36

AN ACCOUNT CONCERNING MOLOKINI

The Hawaiian text and English translation of "He Moʻolelo no Molokini" are from the *Fornander Collection of Hawaiian Antiquities and Folk-lore,* vol. V, part III, pp. 514–519. It forms one of a "series of Lahainaluna School papers," all of them folktales, which are "presented as written" by the students who collected them.

He Moʻolelo no Māui PAGE 40

AN ACCOUNT OF MĀUI

Theodore Kelsey included a verbatim transcript of this legend in a letter to Thomas Thrum dated August 1, 1921. Kelsey's original letter is in the Mele Collection of the Bishop Museum Archives (Hi.M40, p. 8). The Hawaiian text was translated for this volume by Puakea Nogelmeier. This is the first time Hale's legend has been translated into English.

Oli Kūhohonu o Kaho'olawe mai nā Kūpuna mai PAGE 43

DEEP CHANT OF KAHO'OLAWE FROM OUR ANCESTORS

Both the Hawaiian text and Harry Mitchell's English translation of this chant were first published in a 1981 edition of *Ka Makani Kahaukāne*, the Hawaiian language club newspaper of the University of Hawai'i. Mitchell included the following introductory note. "E nā makamaka heluhelu o Ka Makani Kahaukāne: Eia i kākau 'ia ma lalo nei he oli kūhohonu e pili ana iā Kaho'olawe. He oli kēia i lohe pepeiao 'ia i ku'u wā 'ōpio. He oli kahiko loa kēia. Ua lohe paha 'oukou i kēia oli. E 'olu'olu 'oukou, mai ko 'oukou lokomaika'i mai, e ho'ouna mai i kekahi mo'olelo i kēia pepa. No ka mea, he Hawai'i kākou, a he nūpepa Hawai'i kēia, a hiki nō paha iā 'oukou ke 'ike i ka mana o nā kūpuna." ("To those who read the newspaper *Ka Makani Kahaukāne*. Here written below is an ancient chant pertaining to the island of Kaho'olawe. I heard this chant from the lips of my ancestors in the days of my youth. This is an old chant from the beginning of creation. Perhaps some of you have heard this chant. Please, out of your generosity, send a story to this newspaper. Because we are Hawaiian, and this is a Hawaiian newspaper, and so you, the young, can better understand and appreciate our language and culture, and the knowledge of our ancestors.")

Nā Wai Puna o Kamohio no Kaho'olawe PAGE 47

THE SPRING WATERS OF KAMOHIO ON KAHO'OLAWE

Like "Oli Kūhohonu o Kaho'olawe mai nā Kūpuna mai," "Nā Wai Puna o Kamohio no Kaho'olawe" was first published in *Ka Makani Kahaukāne*. Mitchell prefaced the text with the words: "Ke hō'ike nei wau i ka mo'olelo ko'ihonua mo'okahuna kumupa'a a Po'o Ki'eki'e 'o Kamohio, ka mole o ke kumu uli o nā kūpuna no Kanaloa Huli Honua ka pae moku 'o Kaho'olawe." The translation was prefaced with the words: "I am revealing the story I heard from my *kupuna* Kealoha Kū'ike about the high priest Kamohio and of his knowledge of his ancestor's teaching of creation and of the spring waters on the east end of Kamohio Bay on Kaho'olawe."

Ka'ao no Kalaepuni PAGE 52

LEGEND OF KALAEPUNI

"Ka'ao no Kalaepuni" appears in the *Fornander Collection of Hawaiian Antiquities and Folk-lore*, vol. V, part I, pp. 198–204.

He Mo'olelo Ka'ao no Ka'ehuikimanōopu'uloa PAGE 58

THE LEGENDARY TALE OF KA'EHUIKIMANŌOPU'ULOA

The story of Ka'ehuiki's adventures was first published under the title "He Moolelo Kaao-No-Kaehuikimanoopuuloa, Ke Keiki Mano A Kapukapu Ma Laua O Holei, Ka Hoouka Kaua A Na Mano. Hakuia E Mr. William Henry Uaua Esq." ("The Tale of Ka'ehuikimanōopu'uloa, The Shark Child of Both Kapukapu and Hōlei, The Rush to Battle By The Sharks. Composed by Mr. William Henry Uaua Esq.") Its first installment appeared in the November 24, 1870, edition of *Ke Au 'Oko'a*. Subsequent installments continued through January 5, 1871. The selection presented here is taken from *helu* (section) two, which appeared on December 1, 1870, and *helu* three, published on December 8, 1870. Hawaiian orthography was added by both the Hale Kuamo'o Hawaiian Language Center at the University of Hawai'i at Hilo and by Kaleimakana Lenci. Thomas Thrum published a condensed translation in his *Hawaiian Annual* for 1923, as well as in his book *More Hawaiian Folktales* (Honolulu: Advertiser Press, 1923, pp. 293–306). The English translation included here was worked on independently by Hiapo Perreira and Kaleimakana Lenci.

Ka Lawai'a 'Opihi PAGE 62

'OPIHI FISHING

A. D. Kahā'ulelio's "He Mau Kuhikuhi No Ka Lawai'a 'Ana" (Fishing Lore), was published in the Hawaiian language newspaper *Ka Nūpepa Kū'oko'a* from February 28, 1902, to July 4, 1902. A typescript of the original text, as well as the English translation by Mary Kawena Pukui, is preserved in the Hawaiian Ethnographic Notes Collection at the archives of the Bernice Pauahi Bishop Museum.

E Kanaloa PAGE 69

O KANALOA

The *mele* "E Kanaloa" and its English translation are included in Pualani Kanahele's book *E Mau Ana 'O Kanaloa, Ho'i Hou: The Perseverance of Kanaloa, Return!* (Honolulu: 'Ai Pōhaku Press, forthcoming).

Kaho'olawe i ka Mālie PAGE 93

KAHO'OLAWE IN THE CALM

"Kaho'olawe i ka Mālie" is to be published in Pualani Kanahele's *E Mau Ana 'O Kanaloa, Ho'i Hou: The Perseverance of Kanaloa, Return!* (Honolulu: 'Ai Pōhaku Press, forthcoming). The book also describes the Makahiki ceremony as it is presently practiced on Kaho'olawe.

He Ko'ihonua no Kanaloa, he Moku PAGE 97

A HISTORY FOR KANALOA, AN ISLAND

The Hawaiian and English texts of this chant, as well as an account of the ceremony at which it was first performed, will be found in Pualani Kanahele's *E Mau Ana 'O Kanaloa, Ho'i Hou: The Perseverance of Kanaloa, Return!* (Honolulu: 'Ai Pōhaku Press, forthcoming).

MAP OF KAHO'OLAWE PAGE 110

The topographic projection which forms the base for this map was provided by Royce Jones. Place names have been taken from "The Place Names of Kaho'olawe," a report prepared for the Kaho'olawe Island Conveyance Commission by Rowland B. Reeve. These names have been edited by Puakea Nogelmeier, who has added *'okina* and *kahakō* where he felt they were appropriate.

Notes on the Photographers

The four contemporary photographers whose images are featured in this book were chosen for the excellence of their prior work, their ongoing commitment to Hawai'i, and their complementary photographic styles. Their assignment on Kaho'olawe brought numerous technical as well as creative challenges, including such basic problems as keeping their equipment clean and dry. Access to Kaho'olawe is principally by boat, and cameras and film often had to be carried ashore through heavy surf. Once the photographic team reached the island, its only means of travel was by jeep over heavily rutted tracks or by foot, often through areas strewn with shrapnel and unexploded ordnance. Dust was a continual problem, as were the strong winds that sweep across the uplands, often overturning tripods and blurring long exposures. Despite these various obstacles, and in part because of them, the photographers' experiences on the island proved to be extremely rich and rewarding.

WAYNE LEVIN

A resident of Hōnaunau in South Kona, Wayne Levin is best known for his underwater landscapes and photographs depicting the people and peninsula of Kalaupapa, Moloka'i. His work is in some of the nation's finest photography collections, including the Museum of Modern Art, and has been shown in more than twenty-five solo exhibitions, as well as many group shows. He has published *Kalaupapa: A Portrait*, and his images have appeared in numerous books and magazines, including *Mānoa: A Pacific Journal of International Writing* and *Discovery: The Hawaiian Odyssey*.

For his underwater work along the shoreline and in the sea around Kaho'olawe, Levin used a 35mm Nikonus camera with 15mm, 20mm, and 28mm lenses, alternating between Kodak Technical Pan black-and-white film, and Fuji Velvia color transparency film. For landscape photographs, he used a 4x5-inch Baby Deardorff view camera with Kodak Vericolor Professional color negative film, as well as a 35mm Nikon FM camera with Fuji Velvia color transparency film.

ROWLAND B. REEVE

Archaeologist and writer Rowland B. Reeve has wandered and worked in Europe, South and Central America, Melanesia, and Southeast Asia. He brings to his photography both his training in cultural interpretation and an affinity for unexplored places and ancient sites. Born and raised in Hawai'i, Reeve first visited Kaho'olawe in the early 1980s at the invitation of the Protect Kaho'olawe 'Ohana and has spent the last five years studying the island's history and traditions. Some of this research was published in a report for the Kaho'olawe Island Conveyance Commission entitled "Nā Wahi Pana o Kaho'olawe"; more will appear in the companion volume to this book. His knowledge made Reeve the guide for the team as it worked on Kaho'olawe. For his photographs, he used both a medium-format Rolleiflex 6x6-cm, twin-lens reflex camera and a 35mm Nikon FM single-lens reflex. All of his photographs were taken on Fuji Velvia color transparency film.

FRANCO SALMOIRAGHI

Having worked in Hawai'i for over twenty-five years, Franco Salmoiraghi is one of the Islands' most renowned photographers. He has returned again and again to remote parts of Hawai'i—especially to Kaho'olawe, Waipi'o, and Maunakea—making powerful images that distill the essence of these places and the spirit of their people. His work has attracted numerous one-man exhibitions and has been published in several books on Hawai'i, as well as in leading island magazines.

During his early trips to Kaho'olawe in 1976 and 1979, Franco worked exclusively with a Leica M-4 rangefinder 35mm camera using 28mm to 90mm lenses. He photographed primarily with Kodak Tri-X black-and-white film, occasionally with Kodachrome 64 color transparency film. In his more recent work on the island, he carried Canon A-135mm single-lens reflex cameras with lenses ranging from 20mm to 200mm. He used Kodak Tri-X and Plus-X black-and-white, as well as Kodachrome and Fuji Velvia color transparency films. On his recent trips, Franco also carried two medium-format cameras: a Rolleiflex 6x6-cm twin-lens reflex and a Fuji 6x9-cm camera with a wide-angle lens that he used with Tri-X, Plus-X black-and-white, and Ektar 25 color negative films.

DAVID ULRICH

Formerly executive director of Hui No'eau Visual Arts Center on Maui, David Ulrich has been a visual arts educator for almost twenty years, ten of them as chairman of the photography department at the Art Institute of Boston. He was drawn to the Islands to photograph the Hawaiian landscape, and his large-format, black-and-white pictures reflect both the discipline of his visual training and his keen attention to telling details. His accomplishments have been recognized in sixteen solo photography exhibitions and by inclusion in numerous group shows, in several collections, and such publications as *Mānoa: A Pacific Journal of International Writing*.

Ulrich's black-and-white photographs of Kaho'olawe were made on a 5x7-inch Deardorff view camera, using Tri-X sheet film, with lenses ranging from 100mm (extremely wide angle) to 210mm (normal). The contrast range of the images was manipulated through variable exposure and development of the film (the Zone System). His color photographs were made using a 6x9-cm rangefinder camera with a Schneider 65mm wide-angle lens and Fuji Professional 400 color print film.